Tarot for Love & Relationships

Eleonore Jacobi

Tarot for Love & Relationships

STERLING PUBLISHING CO., INC.
New York

Photo credit, page 29: Visum, Hamburg (Lutz Fischmann)

Library of Congress Cataloging-in-Publication Data Available

10   9   8   7   6   5   4   3   2   1

Translated by Nicole Franke and Dan Shea

Published by Sterling Publishing Co., Inc.
387 Park Avenue South, New York, NY 10016
Original published in Germany under the title
Tarot für Leibe und Partnerschaft
© 2000 W. Ludwig Buchverlag, Munchen in the Econ
Ullstein List Verlag GmbH & Co. KG, Munich.
© 2003 English translation by Sterling Publishing Co., Inc.
Distributed in Canada by Sterling Publishing
$^c\!/_o$ Canadian Manda Group, One Atlantic Avenue, Suite 105
Toronto, Ontario, Canada M6K 3E7
Distributed in Great Britain by Chrysalis Books
64 Brewery Road, London N7 9NT, England
Distributed in Australia by Capricorn Link (Australia) Pty. Ltd.
P.O. Box 704, Windsor, NSW 2756 Australia

Sterling ISBN 1-4027-0253-1

Contents

Foreword

Nobody lives an entirely pain-free, totally happy life. We all have our ups and downs and are constantly looking for answers that can help us along — particularly when we are all the way down and it seems, from all appearances, that there is no escape. However, intuitively we know that the more we understand ourselves and our situation, the more we will be able to recognize the sources of a problem, what we have contributed to it, and the better our chances of easing our pain and finding the way to a better life.

Tarot cards present a mirror image of our soul, providing us with information about our past, present, and future. They also give us clues to our emotional life, our attitudes, our anxieties, and our dreams.

Tarot—the Decision Guide

Tarot cards are excellent to use if you're facing a decision that is difficult to make. Not only do they show the possible consequences of this decision, but they also show what circumstances look like in the future. So, if you're facing a change in which you may have to give up something, the cards will bring you the clear awareness that an ending always means a new beginning.

The Tarot Uncovers Backgrounds

Whenever Tarot cards are laid out, they give information about the motivations and the attitudes of the questioner, revealing how much the person is contributing to the problem. Tarot cards, with their pictures, uncover our true feelings and thoughts. They are a mirror of our soul and help us to explore our inner selves.

While they are fascinating, Tarot cards may sometimes be depressing. They hold up a mirror to us, showing the truth to anyone who wishes to see it. The truth I am speaking of is inner truth — that which we believe, that which motivates us and stirs our life. In fact, it is the very motor of our life.

Does He Love Me?

A Question of Love

"Does he love me?" is probably the most frequently asked question of any oracle.

"Does he love me?" is so easy and yet so difficult to answer.

"Does he love me?" is a question that is often a riddle to the questioner.

"Does he love me?" is a question that you can answer with the help of this book.

On the Way to a Successful Relationship

This book wishes to provide you with greater insight into the prevailing feelings in love and relationship. Therefore, the descriptions of these Tarot cards were especially focused on the subjects of love, relationship, and marriage. They describe how we act as partners, how we regard one another, and how we treat each other. We all desire real love and understanding from our partner, no matter whether freshly in love or already a longtime couple. It is to be hoped that this book will help you to see your relationship more clearly, to become more aware of the deficiencies and possibilities of the relationship, and to tackle potential problems successfully.

When partners cannot talk to each other any longer because bottled-up feelings seem to be choking them, the Tarot of Love and Relationships is a wonderful aid in re-opening a dialogue by means of new insights.

7

Tarot—an Introduction

Over the centuries, human beings have time and again created cards with pictures, with which they attempted to predict the future. According to tradition, the first time that money was officially paid for a set of Tarot cards was at the French court of Charles IV in 1392. Shortly after that, the cards were expelled from the court, as they often revealed too much that no one was supposed to know. The origin of the mysterious picture cards, however, is unknown; they may be older still.

> Through their pictures, Tarot cards provide us with a kind of knowledge that is usually limited to our intuition and feelings. They make it possible for us to access an invisible world that contains within it knowledge of ourselves and offers us its help.

A Glance into the Future

In the past, Tarot cards were used mainly to predict the future, and little has changed in this respect. But Tarot cards can do more than that. We live today, as is generally believed, in an enlightened era, but we wonder more and more about our concept of ourselves as human beings. We wish to know how best to structure our lives and why we do the things we do. What causes us, for example, to make decisions that are, despite our better judgment, contrary to our interests? Tarot cards can provide the answers to these questions.

The Invisible World

How can Tarot cards answer our questions and reveal the background of a situation? Nobody can explain this precisely, but it is clear that the statements of Tarot cards are true ones. A possible explanation was given by the American seer Edgar Cayce (1877-1945). While in a trance, he was able to travel to people who were seeking help, to make a medical diagnosis, and then to send these people to the particular physician who was able to help them. When asked how this was possible—for he did not have any medical knowledge—he explained his abilities with the fact that there was a so-called "knowledge pool" or a source of general knowledge, and he had direct access to it after he had fallen into a deep trance. He never needed a spiritual guide.

We learn of similar phenomena in the books of Jane Roberts. This woman, who was endowed with visionary powers, records her conversations with Seth, a spirit who contacted her and gave explanations through her about how the invisible world— the one we cannot see, but which nevertheless exists around us— works. These and other books claim that each one of us is capable of achieving direct access to the knowledge pool.

Cards as Helpers

Since most of us are not aware of our psychic abilities, we have created aids that allow us to access a small part of this immense treasury of knowledge indirectly. The energies that surround us in connection with Tarot cards let us realize, through our unconscious, which cards are significant for us, even if we see them only facedown before us. How would it be possible otherwise to draw as many cards as we like out of a stack of 78 facedown cards, and then receive from these cards a very personal, significant answer to our question?

Individual Messages

Tarot cards, with their information, can be a genuine benefit to our lives, if we are willing to become involved with them. Their message, however, is not transferable to everyone and everything. When you lay out the cards or have them laid out for you, the answers that you receive are valid only for you. If you share your problem with a friend, for example, the advice you get will come from the knowledge your friends have of you. The focus of this advice will be based on the personal experiences of the advisor and not on those of the advice seeker. Tarot cards give answers that are personally

You don't need to possess psychic abilities in order to work successfully with Tarot cards. The knowledge of the cards and their statements are available to anyone who wishes to learn about them.

valid only for the questioner—not for anyone else. The answer is neutral—neither positive nor negative—and it will reveal a situation as it presents itself to the questioner.

Practical Assistance for Life

We have each traced out a path of life, but we don't know how this path is supposed to look. We can get assistance in finding the path through, on the one hand, our inner voice and, on the other, pain. Pain is always a wakeup call to observe our life in greater detail and subsequently to change it.

Although our path may be preordained, we possess the freedom to decide how to shape our lives. It is up to us whether we see in the so-called "strokes of fate" a challenge that we accept, or whether we succumb to fate, on the assumption that we can't do anything about it. The quality of our life is the result of our thoughts. Our personality determines the number of our opportunities as well. A decision or an action brings with it consequences, and we have to bear those consequences until another chance arises for us to make a change. A suitable occasion may not arise for years. Therefore, it is important to weigh your decision carefully before going ahead.

One Example—Living Together

A practical example should help clarify these ideas. Suppose you move in with your partner, though you have doubts and are not certain this is the right move for you to make. But you give it your best shot and hope that living together will work out, although you are not particularly happy. After some time, you have to admit to yourself that you have made a mistake.

Now what? You are again facing a key question: do you give up living together and find your own apartment, or do you stay with your partner in spite of the problems, so that you don't have to live alone? The first decision that you made was against your convictions. Now you are able to recognize

10

THE POWER OF THOUGHTS

this mistake, but you are once again facing a decision that may have serious consequences: either to make a new beginning, or to keep up old habits and live with the resulting dissatisfaction. You need to decide–and maybe the Tarot cards can be of some assistance to you in making that choice.

A Reflection of Reality

There is an inclination to ascribe a lot of negative attributes to Tarot cards, yet the cards do not carry with them good or bad characteristics. Cards we call "negative" may show that a lot of challenging things happened in the past of the person who is seeking advice, or that his life is fraught with great difficulties. It is up to the questioner to regard these indications seriously and, if possible, to take them to heart, and not close his eyes to them.

Tarot cards represent the spectrum of life, but they don't offer value judgments in themselves. They are neutral. All negative, mysterious, mystical, or terrifying forms were assigned to them by human beings who could not explain in any other way the energies that worked through them, or simply did not want to understand them. It is wise for an individual to treat Tarot cards with a lot of respect—but without fear—as they impart universal knowledge about ourselves, which is unique in its own way.

Tarot cards unsentimentally give us information about ourselves. When we are facing a difficult phase, the cards will display these circumstances and connections and will not whitewash anything—even if we don't like the answer.

Hints from the Unconscious

Our journey through life may be adventurous, exciting, painful, and full of joy, victories, and setbacks, and those who accept this view of life have a healthy curiosity. If they live in the flow of life and do not barricade themselves, they can get great fulfillment. We are all on this planet in order to learn, and we all have to find the best way for us to move through our lives. Our unconscious gives us hints about the direction in which we might go. Often this takes place in the form of dreams that tend through their imagery to show us a problem or bring us closer to a solution. In addition to this, we have our intuition, our inner voice, or some other impulse, which may lead us onto the right track.

Problem Solving Through the Tarot

Tarot cards also permit us, through their pictures, symbols, and interpretations, to observe our past, present, and future quite clearly and from a new perspective. Through their information, they provide us with the means to better manage our lives.

Life is an ever flowing stream. Nothing remains as it was. Through our unconscious, we receive indications about how to live our lives. Tarot cards can be a mirror reflection from the inside out, which makes these hints evident to us.

The Tarot of Relationships

Based on the Rider-Waite Tarot deck with its excellent images, the interpretations in this book have been designed particularly for dealing with relationships. The symbolism in the card has not been explained, nor have any general interpretations. Many very good books already do this. Here, the interpretations for each Tarot card refer exclusively to the emotional world. Since Tarot card readings encompass the entire spectrum of life, it is frequently difficult to limit the interpretations of the cards specifically to one area. Usually, a great deal of interpretation is necessary when dealing with relationship issues and their often simple but still very complex misunderstandings. This may make a reading under certain circumstances difficult, but it also sharpens the curiosity for new experiences.

The Validation of the Private Sphere

The cards offer another advantage: relationships are a very personal matter. Even if you discuss them with a very close friend, you may hold back a good deal, as some things are too private to discuss. The Tarot of Love and Relationships allows you to take a closer look at the unspoken problems in your relationship.

Learning to Read the Cards

The Tarot of Love and Relationships, with all its answers, can be a valuable support in all the questions of life. There is no limit to the number of times you may consult the cards, for they point out more than only our future. In addition, it is often impossible to discuss in just one reading all the questions that may come up or to experiment with different spreads. This is, on the one hand, because a session is always limited in time; and, on the other hand, because Tarot readers each have their individual systems with which they prefer to work. Frequently, as soon as the session is over, a crucial question comes to mind that had slipped your mind; and new questions also arise through the answers received.

Realizing and Interpreting Conflicts

The Tarot of Love and Relationships offers you the chance to tackle questions about your present relationship, your former relationships, or your life as a single. In a struggling relationship, you may have lost your objectivity, or you and your partner may be talking past each other. This Tarot will show you your inner inhibition thresholds, what about your partner disturbs you or gets on your nerves, and the unacknowledged anxieties you are carrying around. All these influences affect a relationship and can cause it to collapse. With the help of the Tarot, you can make this conflict clear to yourself so that you can think more deeply about the revealed problems.

The Tarot of Relationships provides information not only about how you think about your relationship, but also how your partner sees his relationship with you. This feedback should not be underestimated.

The Setup of Tarot Cards

Tarot cards are divided into two parts: the Minor Arcana and the Major Arcana. The Minor Arcana consists of 56 cards that are subdivided into four suits—Cups, Swords, Wands, and Pentacles, each with 14 cards. They symbolize the characteristics of the four elements: fire, water, air, and earth.

The suit of Wands represents the creative in us. It is assigned to fire.

The suit of Cups represents feelings. It is assigned to water.

The suit of Swords represents the mind and that which is changeable. It is assigned to air.

The suit of Pentacles represents being rooted to one's native soil, that which is real and within easy reach. It is assigned to the earth.

The Minor Arcana

The Minor Arcana deals with daily life. It shows the different aspects and pictures of life—its joys and also its difficult sides. Cards from Ace to 10 belong to the Minor Arcana, and so do the Court Cards—Page, Knight, Queen, and King. They also express, through their affiliation with a certain suit (Cups, Swords, Wands, or Pentacles) something about the features and character of a person. The Court Cards show us the people who accompany us in life or who play a role in it. When the Court Cards refer to the questioner, they tell something about his or her characteristics.

The Minor Arcana shows us how we master our life; it can be influenced by us.

The Major Arcana

The Major Arcana are the cards of fate. They show our path and the lessons we are supposed to learn. They represent our inner world.

The 22 pictures of the Major Arcana accompany us through every stage of our life, and thus also through all the stages of our love life. The pictures of the Major Arcana are very expressive and easy to remember. The aura of the uncanny or the otherworldly that is sometimes associated with the Tarot cards may result from some cards of the Major Arcana.

The Tarot of Love and Relationships allows you to look at your difficulties very privately and in peace, providing an answer meant only for you. It gives you a wonderful opportunity to think about your relationship without being disturbed by external influences.

- The **Fool** sends us on our way into the unknown.
- The **Magician** shows us that we can rely on ourselves if we have the courage for it.
- The **High Priestess** points out that we should listen to our unconscious.
- The **Empress** sends us creativity and a wealth of ideas.
- With the **Emperor** we can turn these ideas into reality.
- The **Hierophant** is the adviser.
- The **Lovers** indicate that a decision was well made.
- The **Chariot** shows us that we can lead a harmonious life.
- **Strength** teaches us that we possess inner strength, which is at our disposal whenever we seek it.
- The **Hermit** reminds us of our inner voice, which gives us wise advice as long as we want to hear it.
- The **Wheel of Fortune** shows that we are able give our life a positive turn.
- **Justice** is the symbol for cool, unprejudiced thinking, invaluable in making decisions.
- The **Hanged Man** tells us that sacrifices are demanded from us in order to reach goals.
- With **Death,** a new successful life begins.
- **Temperance** points out to us that we are capable of mastering our life with deliberation and compassion.
- We can be successful in our life only if the **Devil** (fear) does not hold us back.
- The **Tower** forces us to conquer fear and to open the door to something new.
- The **Star** implores us to never give up hope.
- The **Moon** represents the unconscious and the often feared mysterious powers that can keep us captive.
- The Moon loses its influence when the **Sun** brings to light the unconscious powers with new vision and positive thinking.
- **Judgment** frees us from old and no longer useful things.
- The **World** indicates that we have closed a circle before we set out upon a new path—as fools once more.

In Buddhism, it is said that the path is the goal. It is pre-

The Major Arcana are the cards of fate. They reflect our emotional life, our thoughts, and the feelings that we experience on our path.

cisely this philosophy that is represented in the Major Arcana.

Reading the Tarot of Relationships

In most cases, cards are laid out for a person who is present, asking a question. The interpretations and answers of the cards then refer to this particular person. With relationships, however, it is often useful to explore how the partner thinks, feels, or regards the relationship.

With the help of the Tarot cards, you can get information about the attitudes of other people even if the latter are not present.

The Six-Card Spread

Years ago, I began to question the cards in regard to the motivation and opinions of people who were not present. I developed the Six-Card Spread specifically for this kind of questioning. and it has proved to be very informative (see page 112). It does not predict a final result, but it does show, depending on the question, how he or she really regards a relationship, a marriage, or even a casual affair. The question "Does he love me?" is, therefore, a good one to be answered with this method. If questions are asked about an absent person, the one who draws the card should know this person. Although this is not obligatory, in my opinion, it brings about a better result.

A Matter of Interpretation

The interpretations in this book do not refer exclusively to the questioner, but also include the position of the partner. Because of that, they are written in the second person. For instance, with the question, "What does my partner think of me?" the opinion of the absent partner is represented as an answer and the cards are interpreted from the point of view of the absent partner.

The Position of the Cards

Two interpretations are assigned to every card in the Tarot of
Relationships: on the one hand, there is an interpretation for
the cards that fall in an upright position, and a complemen-
tary, though opposing, interpretation when the card is
reversed—that is, when the card is lying on its head. Some
Tarot readers regard cards that fall upside down as very negative, but I do not share their view. In my opinion, you draw
the cards that are right for you independent of whether they
fall upright or upside down. You may determine before the
reading whether you would like to read only the upright
cards or also the reversed ones. Let yourself be guided by
your feelings. If a card, however, is turned upside down
during a reading, then it should be read in this way. Reversed
cards are no more negative than cards that are upright, and
are not at all imbued with additional "misfortune."

The Six-Card Spread is an informative, very clearly arranged system. Before turning to the single interpre-tations in detail, let the pictures have an effect on you. What do they tell you?

Interpretation of the Minor Arcana

The cards of the Minor Arcana encompass both a general
interpretation for love issues and an additional interpretation
for a solid relationship. The term "solid relationship" refers
to a marriage or a relationship that has existed for some
years. The general interpretations may also be valid for a
solid relationship, and an additional interpretation may work
for a relationship that has not existed for a very long time. It
is, therefore, a good idea to look at both interpretations in
every case.

Interpretation of the Major Arcana

Since the cards of the Major Arcana describe mainly an
inner attitude, their message is valid for any kind of relationship. However, there is an additional interpretation for a still
very young relationship or one that is just beginning.

Preparation for the Reading of the Cards

Before you begin laying out the cards, decide whether you would like to proceed according to traditional interpretations of the Rider-Waite deck or if you would like to use it only in regard to relationships, as described in this book. In order to use the Tarot of Love and Relationships, no particular ritual is necessary. It is better, though, if you decide on only one structure and get into the right mood for it.

The interpretations of the Minor Arcana take into consideration every kind of relationship—new, already existing, or a long-term partnership. The Major Arcana reflects the inner attitude of the partner. Always have a look at the overall interpretation.

Asking the Right Question

The Tarot does not lend itself to questions that demand Yes or No answers. You might, for example, ask something like "How does my marriage look?" and the cards will answer by dealing with that subject, the circumstances that burden the marriage or support it, and provide a final conclusion. A question such as: "Is our marriage a happy one?" presupposes a Yes or No answer and should therefore be avoided.

Reading the Cards for Others

If you are laying out the Tarot cards for someone else, then you, as the reader, determine the pattern in which you lay them out, and the questioner decides the question that he or she wishes to have answered.

Inner Reverie

Before every reading, whether for yourself or another person, it is recommended that you collect your thoughts. Look for a quiet place and try to relax, becoming entirely calm for the reading. Spread the cards out like a fan, concentrate on the question, and then draw the cards from the pile in front of you.

When Reading the Cards for Oneself

Unfortunately, the rumor has persisted that you should not read the Tarot cards for yourself. Sentences float about such as: "This will only bring about misfortune," "You cannot receive answers," or "One is allowed to read the cards for oneself only once a year at the most," and so on. According to my years of experience, such statements have never proven true. It is, however, possible that you might be so emotionally wrapped up in a problem or a question that it is difficult for you to perceive the connections displayed. Also, wishful thinking can play a role in the interpretation of the Tarot cards, which prevents you from taking note of the statements of the cards if they don't correspond to what you want them to say. This danger always exists.

The posing of a question is very important in the reading of Tarot cards. Tarot cards cannot give Yes or No answers, since they look at the entire happening surrounding the question. They do, however, give you a possible final result.

Getting to Know Your Own Problems

In relationship issues, we usually like to tackle our difficulties ourselves before bringing in a third party and involving them in our problems. The reading of the Tarot cards offers a very good solution. It can help and offer advice without your having to let others know about the delicate subject. The Tarot cards can show you how your relationship is doing or how it looks inside yourself in connection with this relationship. Since the answers that refer to your relationship are not always pleasant and can reveal inner anxieties, it helps if you can read the cards for yourself in order to think about the statements in peace and quiet. Tarot cards always show the essential nature of a question and what occupies or moves us most of all.

Taking Notes of the Cards

Before coming to the actual interpretations, here's one last piece of advice: it is expedient to take notes of all cards laid out. It is very easy to forget what the cards told you and thus lose hints that might be used as important points of reference. Above all, if there is a great deal of emotional pressure, it may be helpful just to take note of the cards and study them in peace at a later time.

It can also happen that the very same cards appear over and over again in different readings. When this happens, the cards are indicating that the subject is playing a vital role in our present life, and we are urged to meditate on the revelations implicit in the cards.

If you wish, you may read the cards for yourself, but always bear in mind that there may be an emotional bond with the question that may prevent you from seeing the answer. For this reason, it's a good idea to write down the positions of the cards so that you can return to them at a later time.

One Example—A New Relationship

After a separation, you may wish for nothing more than a new relationship. In any case, this is what you say when talking with your friends. So you lay out the cards for yourself with the question; "What are my chances for a new relationship?" In the space for your inner attitude, the Four of Cups appears. This card indicates that you are unconsciously rejecting a new relationship. So while you consciously wish for a relationship, you are not ready yet. If you get such a reading, it would be a good idea to focus intently on this statement and think about why you are rejecting a relationship from deep within. Perhaps it is the fear of new pain or the wish for freedom and independence, and you are not looking at that. Tarot cards give hints regarding such ambiguities, offering you the chance to deal with the subject, to become aware of problematic areas, and to make decisions with greater knowledge.

Another Example—Self-Doubt

You lay out the cards, asking about your relationship, and the Five of Pentacles appears again and again, either in the place of the inner attitude or as a Key—or Phase Card. This card tells you that you are jealous and plagued with self-doubt. It is pointing out that you need to become aware of your present emotional condition and this self-destructive

behavior, giving you a chance to change your situation. The
cards certainly don't suggest that you submit meekly to
"your destiny," or cast the blame onto someone or something else. They are rather urging you, through the repeti-
tion of the same cards, to solve the problems you are faced
with.

Minutes of Progress

After you've written down the results of your card readings,
you might want to trace back the progress you've made.
As Tarot cards also display your emotional state, they act
as a good yardstick for whether you have been able to
successfully overcome a negative inner attitude and are
recovering emotionally. You may recognize a change if those
cards that were appearing over and over again do not appear
any more.

Ways of Interpretation

Never hand over your power to the Tarot cards. The role of
the cards is to be of help to you, but they should never
become a crutch. It is dangerous to rely on them too much.
While it is tempting to leave your decisions to the Tarot
cards, this means giving your life over to them. Tarot cards
can be companions and incorruptible advisors, yet the
decisions you make need to come from your own inner
conviction.

Don't Force Things

We often wish for something that we want to get by any
means possible. Let's say, for example, that you have fallen in
love. You pose the question: "Will we become a couple?" The
cards tell you that your chances are not good, but this is not
the answer you wish to hear. Thus, you pose the same question again the next day and the day after, and all of a sudden

If you are looking for a new relationship and nothing works out, the cards can give you answers about how you are blocking yourself.

21

you have the answer that you had wished for most fervently. The only thing is—it doesn't happen. The relationship does not make any headway and the cards do not fulfill what they seem to have promised. What has happened is that the energy that chooses the cards for us is tired of the eternal questioning and, thus gives us the answer that we hope for, even if it doesn't correspond to reality. For this reason, it is highly recommended that you read the cards only once in regard to a particular question. If you want to ask again, let a certain amount of time pass before doing it. Then you won't be forcing answers that do not fulfill themselves.

It does not make much sense to ask the cards the same question over and over again without allowing sufficient time to pass. Impatience will not help you reach your goal.

How to Lay Out the Cards

There are several different methods of shuffling and laying out the cards. The method that has proven most successful for me is described here. No card is chosen as a significator. When it becomes important in a reading to describe the questioner, the suitable card will appear in the right place.

Laying Out the Cards for Yourself

When you lay the cards for yourself: Shuffle the cards as long as you think necessary. If you wish, turn one part of the cards over while shuffling them. Spread the cards out like a fan on the table in front of you, facedown. Draw as many cards out of the fan as are required for the spread you have chosen. Whether you do this with your right or left hand, in my opinion, doesn't matter.

Take the cards into your hand in the same direction in which you have drawn them. Do not revolve them in your hand, as this would change their meaning.

Always lay down the card you drew last below the previous one, so as to maintain the order in which you drew the cards.

When you have drawn all the cards needed from the fan, lay them out in precisely the same order; that is, place the first card drawn in the first position of the spread pattern you have chosen. The next card gets the second position, the third gets the third position, and so on.

Open the cards in your hand like the pages of a book from right to left or from left to right. Never lay out the cards from bottom to top or from top to bottom, as this would distort the meaning of the cards.

Laying Out the Cards for Others

I would like to point out a few fine points, in case you are laying out the cards for others:

Pay attention to the way the questioner hands the cards to you. Make sure they are in the order in which they were drawn. Then lay them out below each other.

Don't forget to inform the questioner of how many cards to draw.

It is of the greatest importance that the cards are laid out in the direction in which the questioner has drawn them. This means that when you sit across from one another, you will have to revolve the cards you have received in your hand from the questioner, by 180 degrees.

The Time Frame of the Statement in the Celtic Cross

You may limit the time frame of your question. For example: "How will my relationship develop within the next three months?" You can set such a time frame for every spread.

In the spread called the Celtic Cross, the period of time for which a reading is supposed to be valid is normally not more than a year. If, however, you pose a general question such as: "Will our relationship develop?" (see the example on page 121), then other indications will affect the time frame. The cards of the Minor Arcana will give these hints: The numbered cards of the suit of Wands symbolize weeks, the numbered cards of the suit of Swords, months. The suit

When drawing the cards, always place one card underneath the other. When turning over the cards, start with the card lying on top and turn the card over like a book page. In this way, you can maintain the order and interpretation.

23

of Cups represents days, but only when they lie next to a card of the suit of Pentacles. The Pentacles stand for years.

When you have laid out the Celtic Cross, look at card number ten and retrace your steps (Card #10, 9, 8 . . .). Do that until you come across a numbered card of Wands or Swords. The number of Wands or Swords on the card will state the time frame. This indication of time has proven very reliable.

The Time Frame of the Statement in the Six-Card Spread

The Celtic Cross provides you with a time frame to which the question confines itself, even if you have not specified a certain time. You may, however, also question the cards about any period of time.

In the Six-Card Spread, you may set up a very specific period of time, such as: "How will my relationship develop in the upcoming month?" Then four of the cards will describe the course of the month, with each card describing one week (see page 120). As this system is very flexible, you can pose a question for any period of time, whether for one single day or for six months.

Interpretation of the Hidden Number

As soon as you have laid out the cards, count the value of all the numbered cards, including those of the Major Arcana. Reduce the sum received to a single digit number. That number will add an interpretation to the statement of your reading that has been hidden up to this point but needs to be included in the overall picture. If, for example, the sum of all the cards turned over amounts to 57, the sum of the digits is 3. This works as follows:

$$5 + 7 = 12$$
$$1 + 2 = 3$$

The hidden numbers have a special significance. Their interpretations correspond to the generally accepted interpretations in numerology:

• **One** stands for new beginnings and determination, but egoism can also be indicated.
• Number **two** indicates common interests, submission, and intuition.
• **Three** speaks for spontaneity, creativity, and a wealth of ideas. It points to the unexpected.
• **Four** means that a goal is realized; this number also has to do with precision, and being rooted to your native soil.
• **Five** speaks of unrest and change; the goal aimed at is difficult to reach.
• **Six** indicates harmony, family, longings, and also sentimentality.
• **Seven** indicates experience, and that the subject is highly charged and needs to be addressed with great tact.
• **Eight**: Self-confidence, organization, cool reason, also emotional coldness.
• **Nine** stand for responsibility, the desire to bring the past to a close, the end, and the new beginning.
• **Eleven** means sensitivity, but also feelings of uncertainty; you do not quite dare to tackle the issue.

Numerology plays an important role in the interpretation of Tarot. When you count together all the numbered cards, you will experience a hidden interpretation of the numbers.

You may have noticed that we skipped a number: the number ten receives the same interpretation as number one because it gets reduced to that number. Eleven, however, is a special number that represents great sensitivity and behaves differently from the number two. For this reason, eleven is treated as a double figure.

Numbers also give information about how you have already progressed in terms of the question or problem. They show whether you are at the beginning of the situation (cards one to three), in the middle (cards four to seven), or whether you are approaching the conclusion of your problem (cards eight to ten).

Overview for Interpreting the Cards

When you lay out the cards, let the overall picture sink in for a while. The pictures in the Rider-Waite deck are very expressive in their imagery, and by just observing them, you can foresee the emotional leanings of the reading. Do not let yourself, however, be frightened by what may seem to you like a negative card.

If Swords prevail in the cards, a lot of things are being handled by reason in this relationship, whereas the feelings are probably kept under control.

With a majority of Cups, emotions determine the relationship, whereas with Wands the lively and unexpected appears in the individuals' life together.

The Pentacles deal with what is material and sturdy in the relationship — all concrete things.

If cards of the Major Arcana are in the majority, something fateful is attached to the question, something that cannot necessarily be influenced by the questioner.

Cards of the Major Arcana also show the inner attitude and things of which you are often not quite aware. These cards can point out what a person needs to learn or change in order to create the preconditions for a successful future.

If cards of the Minor Arcana prevail, you may be able to change the situation much more easily, as these cards describe daily existence.

The cards of the Major Arcana often indicate something fated, which cannot be influenced by us. There are some ways we must go, as we have made the decision to do so beforehand.

When you have turned over the cards, look at them for a little while. Let them sink in. Listen to your inner self in regard to what each card may wish to tell you.

The Celtic Cross is only one possible way to lay out the cards. It tells a lot about the past, present, and future of a relationship.

The MinoR ARcAnA

The suit of Cups symbolizes our world of feelings, our senses, and emotions; it presents the exuberant, but also the unworldly and the ideal. Without these great feelings, love would be only half as beautiful.

As we have seen before, one group of cards of the Tarot deck is known as the Minor Arcana. It is made up of the suit of Cups, the suit of Wands, the suit of Swords, and the suit of Pentacles. The playing cards we use today developed from these suits: Cups turned into Hearts, Wands into Clubs, Swords into Spades, and the Pentacles into Diamonds.

The Suit of Cups

The suit of Cups tells the story of emotions in a relationship: it reports on the highs and lows, the happiness, and the suffering that each of us experiences in the adventure of love. Its players are the Page, the Knight, the Queen, and the King of Cups. All of these are settled in the world of emotions and describe a relationship with regard to feelings, dreams, and fantasies, where things can be sentimental and unworldly.

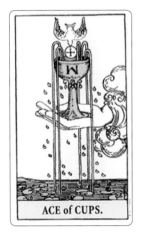

ACE of CUPS.

The Ace of Cups

In general: Freshly in love, you are thinking exclusively about this new experience. The water of the emotions, which causes this cup to overflow, describes it. The cup is held by a hand that appears almost weightless, but it does not fall. It symbolizes the strong feelings that appear out of nowhere and cannot be explained—yet they take over our entire way of thinking and acting. This love is holding you spellbound. As is the case with all Aces, this is just the beginning of a relationship.

In a solid relationship: The Ace of Cups may signify that you have fallen in love in such a way that you cannot imagine life without this new person—even though you might still be in another firm relationship. You may be willing to leave the present partner, yet this separation is, and should be, discussed honestly. Not wanting to be pushed into doing anything, you are not approachable either emotionally or practically. Calls may be ignored or mail left unanswered.

The greater the urging of the partner, the more you retreat.

This card may also signify that you have found the way back to mutual love and feeling in the existing relationship. Maybe there had been a certain kind of indifference, or perhaps the relationship had been taken for granted. Now, however, true affection for the partner may emerge once again.

The Ace of Cups Reversed

In general: What you hoped for in a new partner has not materialized. Possibly, the expectations were unrealistic or set too high. Perhaps the partner acted possessively and left you with too little personal freedom. Wanting to know at all times what the partner is thinking or doing strangles love in the bud; the relationship has little chance to develop. Love does not grow by control, but can only thrive with trust.

In a solid relationship: You are torn between two paths—to leave the partner or not? Love has cooled off; you return home out of sense of duty rather than affection. You believe that the partner can no longer satisfy your wishes. If you have fallen in love with someone else, this card shows emotional conflict. As you still have a certain attachment to your partner, you need to decide whether to hold onto the security of the older relationship and also succumb to the temptation of an affair. This is playing with fire!

People who are too possessive run the danger of suffocating their love. The result is contrary to what they hope for. Love needs air to breathe.

The Two of Cups

In general: With your head in the clouds, each reunion with your partner unveils a shared heartbeat and the feeling of being united. This love comes true like a romantic dream, and distasteful reality is left far behind. You are living exclusively for love in a world to which nobody is granted access except the beloved—a very intense love relationship.

In a solid relationship: You see your partner in a positive light again, just as in earlier times. You may have considered the possibility of separation, but now you are reflecting on earlier mutual interests and the memory of what the partner meant at one time. You are now revealing inner feelings to the other once more, perhaps for the first time in a long while, finding the right words with which to communicate, and experiencing the feeling of love anew.

The Two of Cups Reversed

In general: Although you are madly in love, this feeling is not reciprocated. A first meeting was a diversion without any serious intentions. Even emphatically proclaimed declarations of love are not returned. It is best to avoid forcing promises, since they cannot be kept. There are too few things in common.

In a solid relationship: The relationship is in a fundamental crisis. Serious disagreements appear. Positive feelings disappeared long ago and indifference and frustration have taken their place. One partner reproaches the other, and the mutual dissatisfaction is great. Without new loving impulses, this relationship is in danger of breaking up.

Three of Cups: It is wonderful to celebrate one's love. The promise of mutual happiness hangs in the air.

The Three of Cups

In general: There is a desire to celebrate this love, a feeling that everybody should participate in such happiness. The whole world should know how much in love you are. You only have eyes for each other; the world is rose-colored. This is the stadium of love as it is best enjoyed: romantic without problems, full of optimism regarding the future, with the promise of mutual happiness. Perhaps an engagement is going to be celebrated.

In a solid relationship: Possibly a birth, baptism, or wedding can be celebrated. In any case, revelry will make your mutual love evident to the outside world. You express deep feelings for one another through little attentions, words, or gestures. The relationship is placed under a good star.

The Three of Cups Reversed

In general: The expectations that were placed on the new love have not been realized. Caught up in hard reality, you need to understand that there are conflicted feelings in this love, that you yourself are not the focus of it. You may not want to accept this and may be trying to keep up the facade of "eternal happiness." The relationship is unrewarding and full of problems and tension. Neither partner can remember how nice the beginning was, and neither believes any longer in the promises of mutual love and understanding that were once given. Instead, all activities are focused on unimportant trivia.

In a solid relationship: Daily stress has overcome reciprocated love. Convinced that love dissipates anyway, the feeling is that it would be much too strenuous to put effort into it. Not that you would like to leave the partner or are truly unhappy, but one or both of you have simply become creatures of habit and are now of the opinion that there are more important things than your life together.

The Four of Cups

In general: You want to enter into a solid relationship, but although interested in a partnered life, you have retreated to think over these feelings. Perhaps a former relationship was unhappy and now a new one is being rejected out of fear, because it also might not fulfill what it promises. Or there might be the fear that a new love would interfere with previously set goals. Or you may be aware of a love affair, but not want to see it. You are behaving in a reserved way in order to think about it in peace. Not wanting to be pushed into doing anything, you are not approachable either emotionally or practically. Calls may be ignored or mail left unanswered.

Has your love become lost in the stress of daily life? The Three of Cups Reversed points out that the partner is no longer seen as a lover, but rather as a necessary problem.

31

The greater the urging of the partner, the more you retreat. The urging one had better stop, as you must make your own decision.

In a solid relationship: There is little communication. Daily problems are not discussed, as you prefer to be left in peace. Perhaps professional stress is great and you do not want to discuss it at present. The more the partner tries to force you to talk, the greater the retreat. It might be that you would like to think over these problems first before being confronted with them. A very frustrating condition for both sides.

The Four of Cups Reversed

In general: Willing to get involved in a new relationship, you have become brave enough to show such feelings and throw yourself into the adventure of love, even if it means facing the danger of having to change your life. If you were deeply hurt by a previous relationship and have consequently retreated, you have now recovered, come to terms with the difficulties and disappointments of the past, and found an acceptable solution. Convinced that any future difficulty can be mastered, you feel strong and newly motivated and are facing a new partner with inner conviction, or finding a way to add more variety to an already existing relationship. Common sense is the bedrock of life, as well as a resolve to be more critical regarding the opinions of others. Self-confidence has increased.

In a solid relationship: Right now it is not difficult for you to step out of yourself and to jump over your shadow in order to give the rigid relationship routine a new impetus through honesty and feelings. With serious marriage and relationship problems, you both show the willingness to seek professional help in order to give yourselves a chance to come to terms with mutual problems and establish shared trust once more.

To be urged or to be the urger is the theme of the Four of Cups. One of them retreats and is reachable neither through words nor deeds.

The Five of Cups

In general: Living together has become colorless; there is nothing left to be said and you no longer have the will to invest any further in the old love. You are seeking any excuse to put an end to this relationship. Every separation is connected with sorrow and pain, especially the pain of knowing that your partner will be hurt. Therefore, you hesitate to take this final step. Perhaps mutual opinions and wishes have become so disparate that neither of you can make any sense out of staying together. You have not talked to your partner yet and hesitate, as the Cups in the foreground symbolize the hope that the situation will somehow resolve itself. So, separation is demanded and desired, but has not been carried out yet.

There may be the possibility of an offer regarding a change of location, perhaps for professional reasons, and your partner is not willing to come along. You are therefore of the opinion that the relationship will collapse and are grieving, as it is difficult to accept the farewell.

In a solid relationship: You are thinking of leaving the partner, and the sorrow in your heart is great. Perhaps too many angry words have been said or there has been nothing left to say for a long time. In any case, there is no further connection and you are merely living side by side. On the other hand, it would be wise to reconsider taking this step, because the Cups in the foreground indicate that not all the bonds have been broken and there is still the possibility of saving the relationship. You might be able to find an intermediary who could help build a bridge between the two of you—perhaps a friend or a professional adviser—who would make it possible for you to discuss present difficulties in a sensible manner. The relationship is on shaky ground and needs great mutual efforts to avoid a collapse.

The relationship is inflexible, says the Five of Cups, and is coming close to its collapse. Good will and mutual effort, though, can save it.

The Five of Cups Reversed

In general: You would like to hold onto the relationship. Perhaps there is an awareness and appreciation of what the

33

The Five of Cups Reversed show that you have thought about the relationship. The partners are willing to compromise.

partner means to you. There is a willingness to try your best and show an even greater tolerance. You are ready to accept the partner in the future "as is," although that might not always be easy. A solution for the ever-present problems has been found.

In a solid relationship: The relationship looks more positive than it did some time ago, and you are ready to talk with one another once more. You are daring to make a new beginning, but aware of the fact that this new start will be built upon very shaky ground and that a great deal of mutual effort is necessary to prevent a collapse.

The Six of Cups

In general: This card promises emotional happiness and satisfaction. Love for the partner is at the heart of the relationship and any stand is united. Love has become a firm reality, and the relationship is running harmoniously as the partners work well and share common hobbies and interests. There is also the possibility that a longtime, forgotten love will appear out of the past.

In a solid relationship: Happiness and satisfaction have arrived. The passion has developed into a happy, lovely coexistence; you have learned from former mistakes and are living now in a long-term relationship. There is the remembrance of meeting each other for the first time and you recall with happiness—and perhaps also a little melancholy—the "high" felt in the beginning. Shared responsibilities are split fairly.

The Six of Cups Reversed

In general: You are releasing the past only with the greatest hesitation. You'd like to maintain the relationship as it was in earlier times, but it is unrealistic to believe that the relationship can become that way again. There is the danger that you may put your present partner to flight with so much nostalgia. Your demands upon your partner are too high and unrealistic.

In a solid relationship: Is there perhaps still too great an attachment to earlier times? Perhaps, similarly, you cannot forget your mother's legendary cooking skills, and keep comparing childhood with the present reality. A current relationship is not fostered by dwelling on the past. It is much better to learn to leave the past behind and to concentrate on present and future chances.

The Seven of Cups

In general: A tough decision has to be made: to live together or not? Should we move in together or have separate apartments? You are torn between wishes and expectations and future anxieties. Is this the right partner? Should you really dare to settle down, especially as there is never a guarantee of eternal happiness? All these considerations never seem to lead to any real result. You are only confronted with very difficult decisions that leave you in doubt. As you ponder this dilemma, another fear arises: Will your partner be willing to wait until you work out your answer?

In a solid relationship: You are indecisive about what should be done or even what decision to make. Perhaps there is the question of whether to have children or not, or the choice of having another child. Maybe you are also trying to decide whether or not to take the expensive risk of building a house. All these questions rotate around a mutual future about which you feel very uncertain. Should everything be left the way it is or should you dare something new? Perhaps one partner urges, but the other still needs more time to think it over in order to see things clearly. There is a balance between being against change and not being for it either.

You do not want to let go of the past, says the Six of Cups Reversed. Why is it so difficult to get involved in a new future?

The Seven of Cups Reversed

In general: Once you make up your mind on the path you want to follow, perhaps you will find a mutual apartment and give this new happiness a chance. All doubts have disappeared, and you will put your decision into action with a great deal of energy and optimism. You will be willing to accept that patience, trust, and perseverance are necessary in order to bring a relationship to full bloom.

In a solid relationship: You have finally come to a decision that can be discussed with your partner and are, therefore, willing to do your part for complete success. The time of indecision is over.

The Eight of Cups

In general: Life in its current state does not make sense anymore. Limitation and the feeling of being locked up prevail in the relationship. You are disappointed in life and have not found the happiness that you had been awaiting so eagerly. In seeking new ways for finding truth, it might be necessary to leave your partner behind. Each life is a stream, and there are times when it is necessary to make changes: otherwise, there is a feeling of suffocation. If you suppress these feelings, they will find other ways of manifesting, perhaps through dissatisfaction or illness. An open, understanding conversation with your partner is a necessity.

In a solid relationship: As a couple, you have lived apart from each other in the relationship and do not pursue common interests anymore. It could be that you look at the world in an entirely different light than your partner does, and your individual expectations of life have changed. In order to reach your goal, you must be willing to risk all. It is not clear yet where the path leads, but you know that you have to follow it. This is, of course, will be very difficult for your partner, and it would be unfair to simply leave without

going into the reasons. If you are not willing to face a
separation, then life must be arranged in a different manner.
You need to give up old habits and carry out major changes.
This can mean anything from a new hobby to a new
philosophy of life. This can place a burden on a relationship,
however, if the partner does not comprehend where this
change of mind is coming from.

The Eight of Cups Reversed

In general: You have been living alone for a long time and
are getting ready once more to throw yourself into the
adventure called relationships. Perhaps the frame of conventional norms was broken in the past and a very individual
lifestyle was established even against the will of others.
Possibly the search for yourself has now come to its final
destination. The result of this search may be that you will
expect more from yourself and others in the future. However, you are certainly ready to invest a great deal in a
relationship.

In a solid relationship: You have found a way to dedicate
yourself much more to your individual interests and wishes.
The feeling of finding air once more is nice. Despite many
daily sorrows, you have remained true to yourself, as was the
case before life forced its routine on you. And something has
been gained from this old self. This is not a turning away
from the relationship, but rather a setting free that brings a
new energy and fresh ideas as well as new impulses into the
shared life. Perhaps the boring couch potato is now sporty,
or the old, trodden thinking is relegated to the past and you
are willing to open the door to new things.

The Eight of Cups
Reversed indicates
that you have made a
career for yourself and
are now ready for a
new relationship. You
can bring more into a
relationship now, as
you have grown
inwardly.

The Nine of Cups

In general: You are entirely satisfied with yourself and the
world. And that is not all—you have found a partner you
really get along with and with whom you can share common

37

interests. You are seeing the world through rose-colored glasses; your heart is beating faster because of your joy, and your head is in the clouds all day long. Perhaps this love is celebrated in harmonious togetherness and tender nights.

In a solid relationship: This is a happy relationship. You are living with your partner—and possibly your family—in harmony and unison. A great deal of stability has established itself in the relationship. Love and tenderness come from the heart. All the pains taken to overcome the problems of the past have been amply rewarded. Your life together is full of joy and tenderness.

The Nine of Cups Reversed

In general: Happiness is at stake. Are you perhaps taking things too much for granted? And paying too little attention to the relationship? It would be a good idea to dedicate more attention and mindfulness to your partner and not to be so self-involved. Perhaps you are taking the credit for things, or living too much through your partner. This could scare off your partner in the long run.

The Nine of Cups Reversed draws attention to the fact that you have dedicated your time more to your hobbies than to your partner. Can your hobby really replace your partner?

In a solid relationship: It is recommended that you dedicate more attention to your partner and act more tenderly. You may be giving too much time to other people, and your partner may feel put aside. Perhaps you are occupied too much with work or hobbies, regarding your partner as a subsidiary who should be full of understanding for the activities that actually steal time away from togetherness. Another possibility could be that you are throwing yourself into such diversions in order to escape the togetherness. Frustration and dissatisfaction dominate the relationship.

The Ten of Cups

In general: Happiness has finally come about. The life-partner has been found and the dream of a mutual future will be fulfilled. For the confirmation of this relationship, the promise of faithfulness is given, as this is a love that keeps its promises. The Ten of Cups stands in a rainbow that promises future happiness. Everything works out between the partners —wedding bells may ring.

In a solid relationship: Here is the support and love that is hoped for in a partner. There are many things in common, and one is helpful to the other with problems that arise in professional areas or other kinds. They stand by each other in all matters. In child-rearing, if any, they work together and don't play one against the other. Passion has turned into a deep, understanding love.

The Ten of Cups Reversed

In general: You are no longer willing to give in all the time, although for the sake of peace you have learned to do this. Old problems in the relationship are coming up more often now and remain unresolved. Perhaps you both have forgotten that a relationship is made up of two people and not only one has the say. In case there were wedding plans, they will not be realized now.

In a solid relationship: Family life is characterized by unpleasant tensions and discord. There are many arguments and disagreements between the partners. One partner may be too dominant, and the other may not be willing to give in all the time and may be ready to fight for his/her rights. Children might foster arguments between parents in order to push through their own agendas. It would be advisable to find inner distance in order to analyze the family situation with a cooler head.

The Ten of Cups promises the happiness that is sought so eagerly; yet reversed, the card shows arguments and disagreement, a situation that could be turned into happiness by approaching each other once again.

The Suit of Swords

The suit of Swords deals with mental behavior. These cards are the invisible companions that influence a relationship in either a positive or negative way. They represent the world of

We think, we consider, we have imagination. From this world of thoughts we decide how to see ourselves and our partners and how to act in our relationship.

thoughts that keep you together or separate you. The suit of Swords reveals how your thoughts shape your love.

The Ace of Swords

In general: After a disappointed love or the end of a relationship, you have found the courage to consider taking on a new one. The upward-pointing sword carries the crown of triumph, indicating that the pain from former relationships has been overcome and you are ready to face the game of love anew. This time, you will be led not only by your feelings but also by reason, in order to create a mutually loving life.

In a solid relationship: Finally, you have worked things out with one another, and present difficulties have been overcome. You have made plans to better adjust to your partner and to take his/her needs into consideration. There is now a pleasant new beginning with the certainty that you have taken the right step.

The Ace of Swords Reversed

In general: The old pain over a former love is still present. You are not able to forgive yourself or your former partner. Apportioning blame is very common, but it makes you a prisoner of yourself, and your ability to start anew is denied. In order to make a real new beginning possible, you need to deal with your reproaches and, if possible, forgive oneself and the other person. Until this takes place, a new love will not be realized.

ACE of SWORDS.

In a solid relationship: Games of power are played and you gamble for advantages. Destructive behavior is the main issue here. One partner tries to force his or her opinions on the other and does not respect what the other has to say. Likewise, one partner feels he/she knows each and everything better than the other and tries to gain control. Therefore, the relationship must be considered very much in danger.

Two of Swords

In general: You are thinking about how to deal with a new relationship, but are undecided. How much feeling should you invest in it? You don't wish to discuss your doubts; perhaps you fear getting hurt again and your emotions are hidden behind indifference. You don't feel free on the inside and are determined to do nothing at present but wait and see whether your partner takes the initiative.

Perhaps you expect your new partner to make up for the mistakes of a previous relationship before you make up your mind. You are aware, however, that this behavior is not fair. You are hiding your insecurity behind silence, but a struggle with your true feelings is inevitable.

In a solid relationship: Many things look problematical in this relationship, but you are determined not to discuss them or even to see them. Thus, you remain silent in hopes that all the problems will somehow resolve themselves, though you are surely aware that they need to be addressed. Quite simply, the will to come to terms with the problems is lacking.

The Two of Swords indicates that the problems in a relationship need to be discussed. It is not helpful to pretend that they do not exist.

Two of Swords Reversed

In general: With the readiness to digest the dark points and unsolved problems of the past, the door to a new relationship can be opened up. You realize that your love life has been destroyed through previous negative attitudes. It is not easy to come to terms with the painful experiences of the past, but you feel newly invigorated and are looking to the future with optimism. You are able to draw the right conclusions from the past and to learn from them.

In a solid relationship: Determined to tackle the problems at their core, you bring about a heart-to-heart talk with your partner. The two of you grapple with the matter with cool reason and feelings are kept under control. On the one hand, you are no longer prepared to subordinate yourself to

41

your partner; on the other hand, you are willing and able to talk about present difficulties reasonably, bringing life into a once-rigid relationship.

Three of Swords

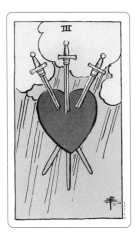

In general: Here the Swords cross right through the center of the heart. You are in love, but ignored by the one you adore. A great deal of suffering results from this indifference, and you are most deeply hurt. No path leads out of this love sickness. Maybe you have fled into a dream world in which everything is all right in order to endure the rejection. The painful step of inner separation is necessary in order to set yourself free of this trap of wishing, hoping, and fantasizing. No relationship can be forced into being, no matter how much love there is. If you are already living in a relationship, this card can signify the separation from an inner attitude that jeopardizes the relationship. In either case, the separation is difficult to carry out.

In a solid relationship: You are not willing to play with open cards. Instead of trying to clarify the situation, you hurt your partner knowingly and without remorse, or your partner intentionally hurts you—a cat and mouse game has begun in the relationship. For both, the joy in things in common has disappeared and what remains are pain and indifference. Whether you are the victim or the culprit, it is clear that the relationship is over. The painful step of separating provides both with the opportunity for a new beginning and indicates a way out of this mutual suffering.

The Three of Swords indicates a painful cut, which is sometimes necessary in order to have the courage to make a successful new beginning.

Three of Swords Reversed

In general: It is difficult to accept that a rejection or separation is final, and one partner may try to get the other back, no matter how humbling this may be, perhaps even through threats or emotional blackmail. But when you finally have the will to let go, you will receive a new chance.

In a solid relationship: Despite all difficulties, the relationship has not been given up. You are willing to accept mental torture rather than face the fear of being alone. Although there are arguments and trouble, you prefer to live in an emotionless relationship in the belief that you cannot make it alone. You know that this is not a good way to live and that constant stress and inner strain can lead to illness in the long run. Self-respect has been lost.

Four of Swords

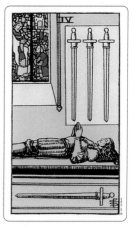

In general: You have retreated in order to have some time to think things over. Should you jump into a new relationship or remain independent? The will to have a solid relationship is not yet fully developed, so you are keeping a certain distance from the possible partner. You are independent enough to decide how to live. Maybe you are retreating in order to avoid coming to terms with an issue. You may be aware that your partner has specific desires that you do not wish to confront, so it is easier to remain silent. In this way, you can avoid unpleasant but clarifying talk.

In a solid relationship: You have completely withdrawn into a shell. Perhaps recently, not everything has worked out the way you had hoped, or maybe there was too little time for one another, or the job and/or the family has asserted itself too strongly in your life. As you are tired of disputes, you need to take some downtime in order to avoid further confrontations and gain strength for upcoming arguments.

The Four of Swords symbolizes inner conflict over the individual's giving up a single life full of freedom. Is the love great enough?

Four of Swords Reversed

In general: You are determined to enter into life once more by escaping from your self-constructed prison. Therefore, you put plans into action with full energy and very little willingness to compromise. You have carefully thought through your ideas and will fight for your opinions as well as your

43

wishes in the future. In addition, you now have the will to face the problems of a relationship without immediately withdrawing into a shell whenever the situation becomes difficult. You feel able to engage in a good fight in order to clear the air.

In a solid relationship: You are facing the problems of the relationship with the certainty that they are solvable. There is a readiness to show more interest in the desires of your partner. If there are children in this relationship, you might spend a weekend without them in order to get to know each other once more. You show more feelings and understanding for your partner.

Five of Swords

In general: There is little honesty between the partners. Either unfaithfulness prevails in the relationship by still feigning love, though romance has not been elsewhere for some time; or plans have been made that do not include the partner, but you are unwilling to say it. It could also be that one of you wishes to compel the love of the other, although the partner shows no interest, or that you are trying by any means to hold onto that love. You may not shrink from hitting on someone else's partner; feelings are being played with, or feelings that do not exist are being pretended.

In a solid relationship: The Five of Swords displays a latent crisis. You are being cheated on or are cheating on your partner. There is dishonesty right down the line: you are being manipulated without being aware of it or willing to admit it. This card shows humiliation and an insidious situation in which you may be victim or culprit. Action is needed in order to break through this pattern and get the relationship back on solid ground. The most important precondition is honesty; only then will the relationship have a chance.

Anyone who manipulates a partner out of self-interest only, is in the end the loser. In such ground, no love can grow and blossom.

Five of Swords Reversed

In general: People often talk themselves into believing that they are incapable of acting or that they cannot manage life alone. Self-esteem, self-confidence, and the will for action have been lost. Thus, you remain in an unsatisfying relationship simply out of fear. Life appears unfair and unjust. If possible, you need to stop deceiving yourself and avoiding problems, but look instead for solutions. In this relationship true feelings of love have not been playing a role, only self-centered interests. You are self-deceived.

In a solid relationship: The notes above are also valid for a solid relationship. You are being manipulated. There is even the danger that one of the partners may make use of violence.

Be more critical of the things others are trying to persuade you about. Here, selfish aims could take precedence.

Six of Swords

In general: Peace has settled at last after the turbulence of former relationships. You have gotten the hang of life once more and are about to build a new future. If you have found a partner, there is the feeling of being protected and in good hands. You are in balance and satisfied with yourself. All barriers are surmounted. You may also move together in order to start a new life.

In a solid relationship: Peace has settled. You have finally had it out with your partner. After the turbulence of the past, love again reflects on what was once so valuable and seemed to have vanished under the burden of everyday life. It is possible that you will make up for the past with a honeymoon or go on a vacation together.

Six of Swords Reversed

In general: Everyday life is full of disappointments and confusion. A more peaceful life would be desired, but you cannot imagine that something like this would be possible.

The Six of Swords Reversed indicates a problem that plagues so many relationships: too much stress, a hectic professional life, and too little time for each other.

You have the desire for a partner, but somehow there doesn't seem to be the time or even the will to establish a relationship. You are burying yourself in work, which results in greater hope and satisfaction than a lukewarm relationship. At this point, your belief in love no longer exists.

In a solid relationship: You know that there is an urgent call for action in order to solve awaiting problems, yet up to now you have made the decision to let things go on as before. However, accumulated tensions are not solved in this fashion. You are aware that a heart-to-heart talk is necessary, but the right place or time can never be found. Or does your partner never want to find a suitable occasion? The relationship does not truly seem to be very difficult, yet there remains the knowledge that things are not perfectly fine.

Seven of Swords

In general: You may possibly be deluding yourself into believing in a love that exists only in your fantasy. You may be reading more into the friendliness of another person than is actually there, and you are not willing to see the truth. Self-deception is the keynote here. You are fooling your partner, as you expect advantages to come from this other situation, or you may be deceiving yourself.

In addition, economic fraud may be playing a role. Do not open your wallet too quickly and generously; show instead a healthy amount of suspicion.

In a solid relationship: You would like to manipulate the partner psychologically in order to maintain a position of power. This could have to do with fraud in financial affairs and other material matters. If you are going through a divorce or have been living separately from your partner, then an attempt may be made to pull the wool over your eyes. It's a good idea to be very cautious and to read every document carefully, as well as to get some competent and educated advice. There may be a scheme to take something to which the partner has no right.

Seven of Swords Reversed

In general: You have stopped deceiving yourself in love and are finally facing reality. You are no longer allowing yourself to be manipulated, and you are convinced of your own worth. If you had previously been unhappily in love, the time has come to find a way out of this lovesickness. The difficulties, from whatever source they might have come, solve themselves. In a relationship that is already over, financial matters are settled justly.

In a solid relationship: An apology from the partner for past behavior can be expected: it opens up the door to new dialogue. If you are the one to whom the apology is directed, diplomatic finesse is needed. If you wish to say something, think about it beforehand; it might be worth the effort to phrase your comments gently and tactfully.

A new way is found to reach toward each other. With a divorce, pecuniary circumstances are settled justly.

You are taking charge of your life once more and freeing yourself of past difficulties and old behavioral patterns. The Seven of Swords Reversed also promises a new impetus in your shared life.

Eight of Swords

In general: You are convinced that you have found the right partner at last; however, you are afraid to take the initiative. There is a feeling of helplessness and uncertainty about what needs to be done. Maybe you are simply afraid of being rejected. In order to prevent a possible rejection, you may prefer to do nothing. But your helplessness is not as great as you may think.

In a relationship: there may be a conflict of interests between the partners, which both face weakly. Both may feel powerless, but they are not. Courage has to be found to overcome this helpless feeling and to bring about clarity.

In a solid relationship: You are not getting any further in this relationship: each dispute circles around the same matters—money, sex, work, or the family. The partners constantly talk past each other. Opinions are rigid and you do not see any way out of the difficulties. You are, however, not

helpless. You have more strength than confidence, so stop allowing yourself to be carried away by your feelings and make a decision.

Eight of Swords Reversed

In general: You no longer wish to stand on the sidelines and have decided to take the initiative and bring about a decision. Furthermore, you no longer wish to remain wrapped up in pipe dreams, but want to take life into your own hands. A contact with the ideal partner is established, and life takes a positive turn.

In a solid relationship: The decision has ripened into a challenge of the unsatisfactory life with your partner. You are no longer willing to give in for the sake of peace, but speak out in favor of your own rights and fight for the survival of the relationship. At last, you are capable of acting once more: you will not knuckle under that easily. Any kind of relation-ship will emerge strengthened from this outspokenness.

Nine of Swords

In general: This card shows the anxieties that plague us so much in love and that usually exist only in our head. You have fallen in love and everything is still new—in fact, everything is wonderful—yet there is a constant worry as to whether this love is returned. Maybe you are racking your brain about whether you will see the companion of your heart again after a hot night of passion—instead of simply taking the initiative. You spend sleepless nights, torturing yourself with doubts and fears, although these wor-ries are useless. The hopelessness exists only in your mind and not at all in reality. The danger is that focusing on these exaggerated anxieties will bring about precisely what you fear. We create our world with our thoughts; therefore, you need to examine your thoughts so that fear is given no life of its own.

In a solid relationship: There is a great deal of worry regarding this relationship, although it is totally unjustified. Perhaps you are persecuting the partner with petty jealousies and unreasonable mistrust, making life difficult. Maybe the partner is often wrapped up in business affairs, has long work days, or is otherwise very much engaged, which takes time away from the relationship and family. It is understandable that this may cause insecurity, especially if the partner does not want anyone else to participate in this work, and does not pay a lot of attention to you. You feel excluded and this, naturally enough, stirs up anxieties. It would be a good idea to make an attempt to reduce such worries with a clarifying conversation.

Nine of Swords Reversed

In general: All previous anxieties have dissolved into air, and now you can't imagine why there were so many sleepless, brooding nights in the past. Possibly a new love has entered your life. In any case, self-confidence has returned.

In a solid relationship: If you are living in a relationship, a clarifying conversation has taken place. Any kind of mistrust was revealed as inappropriate. Perhaps your partner had been so wrapped up in work that he/she was much too tired in the evening to call or go out. Confidence in the relationship is established once more. You have aired your grievances, doubts have been moved aside, and your partner has resolved to let you participate to a greater extent in the workaday life and not to exclude you any longer, as was the case up to this point.

Where previously fear and anxiety prevailed, it is as if these were blown away with the Nine of Swords Reversed. Self-confidence and optimism for the future have arisen once more.

Ten of Swords

In general: At first glance, this card looks as if it's dealing with a deadly injury. In precisely the same way, negative experiences from the past are often still felt in the present. These were difficult times, and possibly a separation had to

49

be coped with. Here, you have not yet come to terms with the past and are still so hurt that you do not feel able emotionally to start anew.

You have said adieu to love. Yet if it is not your wish to destroy yourself in this way, it is important to learn to forgive both the past and yourself. You need to realize that the past has become part of your life, and it represents a gain in experience that you can use in a positive way in the future. If you observe the card closely, you can see the horizon, which shows from afar the promise of a new day. There is a new beginning for everyone, if you are able to let go of the past. Maybe professional advice would help you to release yourself from this mental torment, or perhaps a familiar, trusted person. Of course, there must also be the will to help yourself.

In a solid relationship: You feel deceived and cheated. The separation from the partner was hard and painful. What has remained are bitterness and the apportioning of blame. Yet also in this case, the lightning streak across the firmament promises a new beginning. An ending is always a new beginning as well; you can take advantage of it, if you will.

The Ten of Swords points out that the person has to come to terms with the past and has learned not to carry it around all the time like a heavy package. A new beginning is always possible—never lose hope!

Ten of Swords Reversed

In general: You are aware that you have suffered needlessly, yet you are acting like a masochist who comes back again and again for a good hiding. You want your partner by all means, no matter how badly he/she treats you. Like a boomerang, you keep returning only to receive another humiliation. There is a desperate search for the acknowledgment that you are worth something as a person, but you are no longer able to realize that this is the wrong way to receive an affirmation. For it is this affirmation that your partner consequently takes away, thus increasing his/her power. As long as you allow yourself to be humiliated in this way, there is no way to stop the abuse.

In a solid relationship: You are trying to hold onto a partner by any means, although you know in your heart that this relationship will not get any better. Too many attempts have already been made to save it; the relationship is destructive and hopeless. But it should also be remembered that the family, if there is one, suffers a great deal, too. Children may possibly give you the strength needed to escape the mental morass. You are aware that this suffering has been created by your own indecisiveness. Never give up hope for a better life or confidence in that life. The lightning streak with the promise of the sunrise is present, always.

The Suit of Wands

In the realm of love and relationships, the suit of Wands deals with the creative, the spontaneous, and the mutable. It belongs to the element of fire, which constantly changes, and everything it touches is inspired with enthusiasm. This fire is creative and airy, characterized by ideas and plans. Not all ideas can be implemented in practice, but it is a joy to experiment and try new things. You regard life as a challenge that needs to be explored without limiting yourself to the pragmatic and useful alone. The suit of Wands also describes deeds and business affairs, such as how work and the daily stress of everyday life influence your shared life. People described in the suit of Wands see their new or longer term relationship as an adventure or a challenge and are not necessarily laden with sentimentality. They take part in the happiness of life, but are also willing to fight for their luck.

A relationship thrives on spontaneous and unexpected joys that are mutually offered. The suit of Wands represents this side of the relationship and its creativity.

Ace of Wands

In general: You have fire in your eyes and you are passionately aroused. Full of enthusiasm, you plunge into the promise of a new relationship, desiring only to have the new love reciprocated.

The green that arises from this Wand indicates that you can be confident. You may need to develop a great deal of

51

creativity in order to convince your new love of your seriousness. This is the beginning of love or passion that is dictated by more than just feelings. Here other criteria also play a role: similar views regarding, for example, the planning of leisure time, common inclinations, or the meaning of life. This love relationship has every possible chance of leading into a solid relationship.

In a solid relationship: There is the intention to invest more passion, feelings, and vitality in this relationship than has been there up to this point. Perhaps the decision has been made to pursue common hobbies again, or to go out together more regularly. Common interests and togetherness are being given special emphasis once more. Perhaps, you are even thinking about a common project to which both of you can contribute, or one of the individuals is taking on a new professional opportunity that will influence the relationship in a positive way.

ACE of WANDS.

Ace of Wands Reversed

In general: A new relationship is taken on too fast and too impatiently. With this behavior, the person you long for is more likely to be scared away than attracted. Take more time for your new relationship, instead of being so impatient and wanting too much too soon. Perhaps you have so few mutual interests that communicating is difficult. Even if this is ignored in the first intoxication of love, it is nevertheless an important point to consider if a relationship is to continue to develop on a sound basis. Without this commonality, the relationship will not click.

In a solid relationship: The desire to get a life going that is shared with the partner has remained unrequited. It could be that your expectations are set too high, and thus cannot be fulfilled by your partner.

Impatience and a strong desire are more inclined to put a new love to flight than to attract it. Try to develop more patience—that is what the Ace of Wands Reversed points out.

Two of Wands

In general: You have sent a message to the person of your dreams. This is a hazardous enterprise for it is uncertain how this thrust will be received. You do not know very much about the one who has stolen your heart, not even whether he/she is single or deeply involved in another relationship. But you will dare the adventure, confident that the enterprise will succeed. New plans and connections promise to work out.

In a solid relationship: You feel comfortable in this relationship; each partner complements the other well; there might even be shared professional plans in the future. The card tells that the final ending is not determined yet, but that the partners have enough self-confidence to tackle these mutual goals successfully.

Maybe you have been put off too much by a supposed rejection by the partner, without being sure whether this rejection actually exists. You may be plagued with old and unresolved relationship problems that you have carried over to the new partner. Unconsciously, you have weighed each word of the partner and found it not good enough. You might ask yourself whether this judgment is justified, or whether you expect the new partner to recompense you for previous events.

Two of Wands Reversed

In general: Like a turtle, you have withdrawn into a shell and dare not make any advance toward togetherness. Insecure, you doubt that a serious relationship will come into being with the partner desired. Perhaps you have even let the contact fall away because your self-doubts are too great.

In a solid relationship: Serious doubts have sneaked in as to whether this relationship is still working for you. You are faced with too many discrepancies between what you want

The Two of Wands Reversed represents the self-doubts with which you try to come to terms, without talking to your partner. Does he/she love me or not?

53

and what the relationship is providing, and you have not made a serious attempt to clarify the problems. The partnership has developed into one of convenience in which each plays only the part assigned. If the two of you once considered making professional plans in common, they are now put on hold for the time being. One of you has changed his/her mind or might not be willing to take the risk in this critical situation.

It is important to enter into a dialogue with the partner, even if this is difficult, in order to find out exactly where the problems lie.

Three of Wands

The Three of Wands promises that a phone call, a letter, or an e-mail has arrived. He/she has gotten in touch with you. Mutual understanding and respect prevail.

In general: If there were once doubts about the partner or the new relationship, these irritations have now been dismissed. If you have established contact with the ideal partner, you will receive a positive answer. The partners get along very well and are able to have great conversations. Mutual difficulties are discussed and solutions for problems are found. There are a lot of common interests.

In a solid relationship: You are willing to work together to find a solution when facing a difficult time. Each of you expresses your point of view very clearly without being hurtful and is willing to participate in discussions. You will also listen to and accept the opinion of other family members. When dealing with professional issues, you also find the support of the partner.

Three of Wands Reversed

In general: In this relationship, the willingness to communicate has hit rock bottom. You give or receive only answers that do not communicate anything; not a single topic is addressed seriously. When a dispute arises, you refuse to give in or even to listen to the partner in peace. Maybe you are secretly hoping to teach the partner a lesson in this way. This has become a risky game that could burn your fingers.

In a solid relationship: The initial vitality and enthusiasm have vanished, and there is no longer a common point of communication. Each partner continually talks past the other. The partners are scarcely in the same boat any longer, as you each wish to fulfill your plans alone without including the partner. Instead of any kind of communication, the following motto seems to prevail: "Either you do what I say, or I'm going without you." You each insist on getting your point of view across no matter what. It's also possible that no conversation takes place at all and there is just an icy silence. The relationship suffers a great deal from this type of behavior. It would help to get clear about exactly how much this relationship still means to the partners.

Four of Wands

In general: A partner has been found with whom you are extremely happy and feel closely bonded. Perhaps you wish to move in together. The time that you spend with each other is marked by love, tenderness, and common interests. Perhaps you like to dance or share another hobby. Both of you are aware that this relationship is more than just a promising beginning; you are very serious about its working out. Everything is directed toward the future with optimism.

The Four of Wands promises mutual happiness and a lot of tenderness. Maybe an addition to the family can be expected. You both look forward to this very much.

In a solid relationship: You are looking forward to a possible addition to the family. The relationship stands upon firm ground; the partners understand each other and know what they can expect from the other. The interplay of family affairs and professional duties is well balanced, and it is okay for one of you to come home from a stressful workday—at least once in a while—in a less than pleasant mood. Understanding and compassion are waiting, so the way home is a pleasant one.

Four of Wands Reversed

In general: Difficulties arise in this relationship. Life together has not developed as harmoniously as you had hoped. Maybe you have realized that your partner's ideas do not correspond to your own, and it is hard to accept this fact. Possibly, you are attempting to remodel the partner according to some pre-existing expectations. Such an attitude will have little success, as this is trying to do the impossible.

In a solid relationship: There are differences that lead to constant skirmishes. The occasions may be very banal and mundane: perhaps you cannot come to an agreement in regard to the division of labor in the household and therefore, one of the partners feels exploited and unable to cope. Disagreements might also arise about leisure-time activities. The partners cannot get through to each other; neither one wants to give in. You might reconsider your own attitude toward giving and taking. The partner cannot be bent into the "right shape" according to your pre-existing ideal, but must be granted independence.

> Do constant arguments about each and every chore in the shared household really create a pleasant life? The one who wins these skirmishes may nevertheless be the loser in the end. The Four of Wands Reversed asks us to think about it.

Five of Wands

In general: An attempt is being made to impress other people, to present yourself as more important than you actually believe you are. In a young love, the person wishes to play the strong one in order to leave a favorable impression. In a relationship, the attempt is made in order to gain supremacy. Perhaps you believe that you show weakness by accepting the partner's opinion and agreeing with it. It is difficult to give in for fear that something might be given away.

In a solid relationship: One argument follows the next. In order to wear down the partner, you bring on ever new conflicts, although they concern nothing really important. Your claims are met with little sympathy from your partner and are made for only one reason: to prove that only one person has the say-so—and that is you. This behavior shows a narrow-minded attitude that has led to problems. Your life together is shaped by your differences.

Five of Wands Reversed

In general: You are not fair in dealing with your partner. You are fighting by using dubious means—emotional blackmail and scurrilous tactics. Anything goes in order to achieve the desired goal. You do not recognize the rights of your partner, feeling that you are always in the right and must prevail.

In a solid relationship: Here, we are dealing with the issue of supremacy in the relationship and in the family. You do not even shrink from pulling the children into the struggle. This is a mean game and unfair toward both the partner and the children. Every human being has the right of self-determination, and this must be granted to a partner in marriage, yet you are not willing to accept this fact.

Each partner has the right of self-determination, as the Five of Wands points out; one person, however, does not want to allow this right to the partner. This fact puts a great burden on their life together.

Six of Wands

In general: The ideal partner has been found and perhaps even won —in spite of tough competition. You stand behind this relationship and are proud of your conquest. There is immense happiness, and you look into the future with great confidence. Difficulties belong to the past. This card may also indicate a marriage proposal.

In a solid relationship: You are extremely satisfied with yourself and the relationship. Everything that you have previously worked for now bears fruit. Past disputes have been settled, and mutual understanding and a harmonious relationship have been brought about. It is also possible that an addition to the family has arrived, and you are full of joy about this. Everything has worked out just fine. Perhaps the children have passed their final exams in school or come of age. This is the time when the goals you set have been achieved.

Six of Wands Reversed

In general: Somehow nothing is really moving along any-more. Life with your partner has become inflexible and turned into a boring habit. What prevails is an inexplicable dissatisfaction, as there is actually no concrete reason to complain. Everything seems to be taking place as usual—but something is missing. Maybe you are too sure of your partner and are not taking great trouble these days; or you are no longer willing to invest any work in the relationship. Passion needs to be rekindled in this relationship. One of the partners has to take the first step; therefore, do not wait for the other person to take the initiative. Perhaps it has not yet even caught the attention of your partner that things are not going as well as in earlier times.

The relationship is lacking in passion. The Six of Wands Reversed asks for more effort. Do not wait for the partner to take the initiative, but do it yourself.

In a solid relationship: Here you have been having a row. A general feeling of frustration and dissatisfaction prevails with your situation in life. This may not have anything to do with the relationship, but it is nonetheless transferred to the partnership as well. Perhaps an expected promotion has not taken place or the children have not passed their exams. The ideas you hoped for have not come about. If plans are made to build a house or to move, there will be delays. Cohesion is needed in order to solve accumulated frustrations and problems.

Seven of Wands

In general: You need to defend yourself against suspicions that you have cheated on your partner, or you may be, in fact, the one who expresses these suspicions. Perhaps somebody is trying to come between the two of you and is spreading these accusations.

If there are professional difficulties, perhaps through envious coworkers, it would be a good idea for you to discuss them with your partner, as the bad atmosphere or a depressive mood could be misunderstood. Mistrust or hidden accusations gain ground and burden the relationship. It is much better to call these problems by their proper names and thus, bring about clarity. If you have to fight for your partner, your chances of winning are good. However, don't be confused by false friends or bad advice; rely exclusively on your own instincts.

In a solid relationship: Mistrust is sown. Somebody is trying to drive a wedge between the partners. The suspicions might have come from envious people in your immediate surroundings, or perhaps from in-laws who come between the partners and wish to sow seeds of discord out of self-seeking interests. There is still a very good possibility that you will successfully defend yourself against such attacks.

Seven of Wands Reversed

In general: If you have fallen in love, this love will not be fulfilled unless you take the initiative. Restraint is often mistakenly understood as disinterest. Perhaps you can be more proactive. The chances of the relationship becoming more solid are not good unless you are willing to work on it.

In a solid relationship: Someone wants to interfere in the relationship, yet you retreat and hope that the difficulties will disappear all by themselves. As you are not willing to discuss your concerns and fears, but rather give the impression of indifference, your partner will misunderstand your behavior. Then it will become an easy game for third parties to stir up dissatisfaction between you.

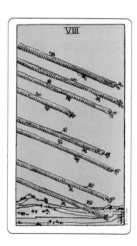

Eight of Wands

In general: Personal freedom is being defended. Actually, you are not disinclined toward a relationship—as long as there is no feeling of being shut in. To you, free space is vital, and you must be able to pursue your own interests even without the partner. This is, of course, very difficult for the success of a love relationship, especially when the partner

The Eight of Wands shows that some people cannot live without their personal freedom. This makes them very insecure partners. The nearest hint of enclosure causes them to fly away.

does not understand this urge for freedom. It may need a good deal of explaining that this behavior has nothing to do with a lack of love, but that you cannot live with the feeling of being locked up.

In a solid relationship: You are continually fighting for the free space that you feel is vital. You must be able to do things outside the relationship, alone. You cannot tolerate being tied to the partner's apron strings, and it is only with great difficulty that you are able to put up with any kind of schedule at all. It is necessary to explain these feelings to your partner with a lot of loving care. If the partner does not understand it and tries to take away your freedom, this will cause the relationship to collapse.

Eight of Wands Reversed

In general: You have the feeling that the relationship is too restricting. The limits are experienced as so narrow that they cannot be dealt with. This kind of constraint appears unreasonable. The prognosis for a shared future is not good.

In a solid relationship: There is the feeling of oppression, and a lot of frustration and antagonism toward the partner results from it. Although you try to mark out greater personal freedom again and again, it doesn't happen. There seems to be no way to make these wishes heard—they are ignored and brushed aside as unimportant.

The Eight of Wands Reversed has turned the relationship into a prison cell; at least, this is how you experience it. Is there any possibility of your being granted more freedom?

You have, however, allowed this restriction to take place, and have entered the relationship in hopes of convincing your partner of these needs as soon as the relationship has become more solid. It would have been important to speak about it honestly from the very beginning and to take the views of the partner into account. Neither of you can change the other, but only understand him/her. Now the matter seems to have gotten stuck: you cannot find a way out, although you still see your partner as very attractive. In the meanwhile, the relationship seems like jail.

Nine of Wands

In general: With a new relationship, the same problems will arise that caused the previous relationship to collapse. The Nine of Wands indicates that nothing has been learned from former experiences and old mistakes are repeated. It is possible that, resulting from your own great fears, too great demands are asked of the partner which he/she cannot fulfill. Perhaps you expect that the partner is to be your consolation for the suffering you experienced in previous relationships. It would be a good idea to examine your attitudes critically and analyze why the former relationships failed to last.

It is also possible that you lack the necessary consideration for the needs of your partner, since it seems that you feel it is of greater importance for you to push through your personal agenda. What prevails is an imbalance between expectation and fulfillment.

In a solid relationship: The partners fight again and again because of the same old problems. For some time there had been peace, yet all of a sudden unresolved difficulties have arisen once more and are waiting to be dealt with. There is a feeling of helplessness, for you had hoped these problems would sooner or later be resolved. However, everything that has been swept under the rug appears time and again, and it will until someone is willing to tackle the matter. This card asks that you discuss with your partner the things that affect him/her, as well as what is so irritating. If possible, keep this discussion free of reproaches, because only a conversation led by reason will help you find a way out of the difficulty.

The problems in a relationship move in a circle, and the very same problem appears again and again. The Nine of Wands asks us to consider why expectation and fulfillment are not brought in line.

Nine of Wands Reversed

In general: One of you seems to be unwilling to admit that you are contributing to the tensions in the relationship through your actions. You are always accusing your partner. There is a great inflexibility here that may bring this relationship to the brink of collapse. You insist on being right even if faced with the evidence of your own actions.

In a solid relationship: You are not willing to talk about problems or to make an attempt to resolve the conflict. You insist on always being right and that no further efforts in service of the partnership are needed. Such overbearing behavior does not lead to a close relationship. You may continue only living side by side.

Ten of Wands

In general: In a still young relationship, you may have a difficult time trying to satisfy the demands of the job, leisure time, and the new love. You may have a feeling that you are unable to handle things, and that the demands of the other person are bothersome and insensitive. You are not only stressed and possibly even impatient, but you may also reach your personal flashpoint very quickly, full of rage toward your partner.

In a solid relationship: You feel absolutely overwhelmed: you have taken on the responsibility for the shared life and nothing remains for the other person except to adjust to it. You are dissatisfied, but don't know how to defend yourself, and you've run out of energy for it. It would be worth a try to work out a better division of tasks—unless you are insisting on doing everything yourself.

You are overwhelmed with work, family, and the demands of the partner as well as the duties of everyday life. The Ten of Wands tells us a better division of tasks between the partners could be a solution.

Ten of Wands Reversed

In general: A promising partnership is entering into a crisis and may not survive the first conflict. One person feels too much under pressure and cannot cope with it. Perhaps it is you yourself who is limiting the partner with such things as constant demands for an affirmation of love. Perhaps you have taken refuge in addictive behavior—food, alcohol, or other things. Try to hold back a bit so that you don't bring about the failure of the relationship.

In a solid relationship: The individual has thrown in the towel and is convinced that the relationship has collapsed. An unjust splitting of roles has caused its failure and you yourself could be either victim or culprit. If you are still interested in saving the love relationship, then it is quite necessary to undertake something constructive.

The Suit of Pentacles

The suit of Pentacles deals with material things in a relationship—money, things you have worked for. The suit of Pentacles represents the financial and practical side of life. What you can see, feel, or touch is very important in a relationship. The suit of Pentacles does not build pies in the sky, but solid houses, just as you do not live in dreamland, but transform your ideas into reality. A relationship must hold water—you want to know where your journey with your partner is supposed to lead and how it will look when it gets there.

Material things are also very important in a relationship. The ability to agree on common goals often determines the success or the collapse of a relationship.

Ace of Pentacles

In general: In a new relationship, you need the patience and inner peace to allow it to grow slowly. You need to be convinced that you've found the right partner, and you need enough self-confidence and self-assurance to prevent yourself from being pressured into anything. This love is founded on mutual trust and understanding and is not dependent on passion alone.

In a solid relationship: Your life together stands on a good foundation. You've worked very hard on this, and a sound, financial basis has been created. The relationship blossoms with mutual love and understanding, and it is founded on solid fundamentals.

ACE of PENTACLES.

Ace of Pentacles Reversed

In general: Hopes for a solid relationship have not come true. You have the feeling that the rug has been pulled out

The Ace of Pentacles Reversed shows the inflexibility that some people allow to dominate their lives. It's hard to be spontaneous, but it might do the relationship a lot of good.

from under you, and the world no longer makes any sense. Perhaps you have tried too hard and always sought to regulate and control each and every aspect of life. Possibly, your individual lifestyle and basic idea of life are not compatible with those of your partner.

In a solid relationship: You may plan everything well ahead of time, but this is not always a sound thing to do. You may already know at this point where you will be spending your next vacation twelve months away. Spontaneity is completely lacking. The activities of life have become rigid, and it is difficult to deviate from your usual lifestyle. Love runs the danger of being suffocated in the routines of this relationship.

Two of Pentacles

In general: Career and relationship are more or less in balance, so you feel satisfied. If necessary, compromises may be made so that neither one falls short. You are in the fortunate position of being able to reconcile everything in your life. As a partner, you are very reliable, if sometimes perhaps a little transparent. Despite that, and beyond sound feelings for your partner, you have not forgotten the practical side of life. Perhaps you need to incorporate a few new surprises once in a while, and leave the well-traveled paths in order to explore new impulses.

In a solid relationship: You are dealing with both the requirements of work and the demands of the family. Mutual finances are being run effectively. This card represents flexibility in a relationship and shows that you are capable of adjusting to the wishes of your partner. There is mutual respect and confidence.

Two of Pentacles Reversed

In general: Here the economic status of the partner is most important and comes before all other values. One of you is deluding the other into thinking that there are feelings where there are not, in order to fulfill a personal agenda. True love is not at stake. The relationship is more concerned with the maneuvering of the feelings and emotions of the partner.

In a solid relationship: Here is a relationship of convenience where economic interests are the top priority, not feelings for the partner. The life shared lacks incentives, for there is little to talk about and few common interests that reach beyond the materialistic. One partner may be staying with the other because financial security ranks above feelings. Or there may also be the fear of an independent new beginning.

Here personal economic interests are top priority and you are not inclined to let feelings interfere. They are rather a means to an end, says the Two of Pentacles Reversed.

Three of Pentacles

In general: You are regarding the relationship optimistically and already working diligently on the future. Perhaps, a savings or trust fund has been opened in order to place the life shared on a solid economic basis. Although the Three of Pentacles indicates that you can place a certain amount of trust in the future and the partner, it would be a good idea not to rush things, but to speak first with the partner about his/her plans. Perhaps, the partner wants to get to know more of the world before getting into a firm relationship and settling down. Try to keep sight of your partner's needs aside from your own enthusiasm. Deep love is felt for the partner.

In a solid relationship: Together the couple works on the future. Perhaps a house is built or a condo bought. After hard labor, the family shall now stand on a secure, material foundation. You can approach such a project with confidence.

Three of Pentacles Reversed

In general: Nothing has developed in the way that it had been imagined. The future was firmly planned, but not one of the wishes and expectations has come true. One partner has neglected to include the other in the plans. It is vital to sit down with the partner before decisions are made and not to

One partner has things firmly under control and decides how life in the relationship is going to be, as the Three of Pentacles Reversed points out. What's lacking are conversations with the partner and listening to them.

exclude him/her any further.

In a solid relationship: One partner is making all the decisions alone without including the other. Discussions and open contact with one another are missing. Therefore, this relationship is very one-sided. Perhaps the partner would like to know how a plan for vacation, a possible move, or a family project is going to work. Keep in mind that the partner also has very particular personal ideas of the partnered life and should not be confronted with a *fait accompli*. Otherwise, he/she might have to realize that the relationship has taken a very unsatisfactory course.

Four of Pentacles

In general: In a relationship that has just started, feelings are locked away in the closet, since you want to be sure first that the new partner returns them. But how can the partner do that if he/she does not know about these feelings? This is a question that you might ask of yourself. This non-communication can make a relationship wither.

Perhaps you have established something together with your partner, but now doubts have arisen that cannot be put down. There is no real happiness in the way the relationship is developing, but you don't see any way of changing this condition. There may be too much rigidity and routine, or perhaps you are not perceiving the true wishes of the partner. It is becoming difficult to accept new things or to change your attitude, even if it would be of benefit to the relationship.

In a solid relationship: Only one partner is determining the path of the shared life and with it the common future. This person has gained supremacy in this relationship and is not willing to become more flexible and to listen to the other. As a result, something is missing. If an individual is not willing to allow spontaneous feelings and take risks once in a while, a relationship will become dull. The supremacy of one partner suffocates the relationship and the dominating

partner will not receive the love that he/she seeks, despite any amount of control.

Four of Pentacles Reversed

In general: You are very possessive and do not want to stop clinging. There is such great insecurity—such fear—that no freedom can be granted to the partner. Through this behavior, a relationship will enter into very great difficulties.

In a solid relationship: You are trying by any means possible to force your will upon your partner. Rejection and disputes are the result, and this seems to justify you to an even greater extent in imposing your will. It would be good if this vicious circle could be broken. You need to seek out conversations with your partner and address those fears, though you may be of the opinion that this is unnecessary, since the partner is to blame for these recurring problems. This may reinforce the decision to do nothing to change the situation.

Five of Pentacles

In general: Jealousy plagues the partners, and self-confidence has been struck a hard blow; thus, an attempt is being made to bind the partner to yourself above anything else in the world.

You may be believed that the partner is cheating, and not want to listen to anything to the contrary. Tortured with self-doubts, you attempt to gain self-confidence through the partner and to make him/her responsible for your misery—this self-destructive behavior can only cause a relationship to collapse.

In a solid relationship: Unreasoned jealousy will destroy everything that has been established up to this point. You—the jealous person—should question why you lack self-confidence and try to get to the bottom of that great morass of mistrust. The relationship is on very shaky legs, as you are hiding your feelings and no longer sharing them with your

Anxiety makes it impossible to relate openly with the partner. One person seeks refuge in a dominating fussiness and pins the blame on the other whenever things do not work out right. The Four of Pentacles Reversed indicates that such behavior can only provoke disputes and disagreements.

partner. Jealousy is no proof of love and should not be regarded as such; trust, on the other hand, is the only evidence of love.

Five of Pentacles Reversed

In general: A relationship has collapsed under the pressure of jealousy and unjustified accusations. You are convinced of the fact that only continuous control can assure the faithfulness of your partner. Solemn declarations of love are not believed and when the partnership fails, it will be taken as a confirmation of these feelings. You do not realize that your own mistrustful attitude has been a primary cause of the collapse of the relationship.

In a solid relationship: Jealousy cannot be bridled and you are pursuing the partner with accusations and suspicions. You are completely out of joint. The sought for relationship has long since stopped existing and love is no longer available in this partnership.

Here the harmony is found that has been longed for in a relationship. There is a strong, understanding, and loving partner, says the Six of Pentacles. This portends very well for a common project.

Six of Pentacles

In general: The relationship is running very harmoniously. It's as if the two of you had been searching a long time for each other and finally found what you were looking for. You seem to be walking on air; your happiness can hardly be grasped; and you are organizing the time spent together as beautifully as possible. Self-confidence and strength shape the relationship: you are as steady as a rock and support the partner with loving dedication.

In a solid relationship: You are happy with your partner and willing to contribute to a harmonious life together, often surprising the partner with little presents. The common finances are right, as are plans for the future. If you wish to build a house or would like to apply for credit, the right time has come.

Six of Pentacles Reversed

In general: In this relationship, the roles are very unbalanced. Your partner expects everything to be organized for him/her in terms of the joint life. You are willing to work hard for the relationship, but are receiving more criticism than praise. Even though your partner has not contributed anything essential to the relationship, her/she is frustrated. This behavior can get on your nerves. Recognition and support are missing.

In a solid relationship: You feel forced to take on the responsibility for the relationship alone, and thus feel exploited. Even if you complain, nothing happens, because nobody in the family pays any attention to the efforts that are performed for others. You are slowly but surely getting sick of always working yourself to exhaustion for the family or the partner without receiving any recognition.

Maybe the partner even knows that you are longing for appreciation and holds this back in order to maintain a more powerful position. If you wish to bring about a change, think over your own attitude and take the necessary steps to resolve the situation.

Seven of Pentacles

In general: You are interested in another possible partner, but uncertain as to whether to get involved. If you like being single, you fear the unrest and disorder that a more solid relationship could bring into your everyday life. It may be that still another relationship is in play that you do not wish to give up, even though the new one is challenging and engaging. Even if an existing relationship is dull, you still value it. It's difficult to give up old and familiar things; yet a decision has to be made sooner or later.

In a solid relationship: The question arises as to whether the relationship still makes sense. The partners are living side by side without truly interacting any longer. The security that

The Seven of Pentacles confronts a person with a difficult decision: whether to give up the old lifestyle, and perhaps the old partner, and look for someone new—habit against risk. How to decide?

this relationship offers is, however, still a very important element. Fear of being alone causes both to make compromises.

Perhaps you are also afraid to lose material security. Children too can play a role in why this relationship continues. Consider carefully whether the loveless partnership is a good one or whether children might start to suffer under such conditions.

Seven of Pentacles Reversed

The Seven of Pentacles Reversed says that you are ready to give up old habits and to face the challenges of life. You feel reborn.

In general: You have decided upon the partner and are willing to give this love every chance for success. There is a determination to lay aside old habits, if necessary, and to face the challenges of life and of love. Joyful expectations and optimism prevail, along with the feeling that this time everything will work out fine.

In a solid relationship: You have decided to follow new paths and are ready once more to get thoroughly involved with the partner in order to straighten out the shared life or, if it has to be, to dissolve the relationship. You don't want to spend your life without love and tenderness. The decision to act has been made, and you are willing to bear any consequences resulting from it.

Eight of Pentacles

In general: The Eight of Pentacles promises only good things. You may have found a partner after a long period of being single, and are daring to try a new relationship, although you had already given up hope for a happy one. You have enough life experience to know that you must contribute to a successful relationship. Great changes will be in store, but there is the willingness to learn and adapt. You had not thought it possible to fall in love again.

In a solid relationship: A lot of things have taken a turn for the better, and a fresh breeze is entering the relationship. Perhaps the children have left home and you have more time for love and tenderness. You discover each other anew, leaving old and rigid paths behind and setting out on new ones. If professional plans play a role, a new stage of life is about to begin here as well.

Eight of Pentacles Reversed

In general: You expect more from the relationship than the non-risky love play that you have been dealing with up to now. The lack of commitment that has distinguished this relationship is hard for both to endure; however, you may not want to admit this, so as not to provoke any conflicts. You accept this situation in the hopes that it will change all by itself one day.

You had long ago given up hope for a new love and adjusted to a single life, yet all of a sudden it is there. Life looks new and promising.

    In a solid relationship: This relationship does not necessarily deserve that name, for it is much more a casual living together. Each partner goes his/her own way. Neither partner is happy with the situation, but neither one knows how to change it. Perhaps one of the partners has an inflexible routine and cannot imagine setting out upon a new path. It is time to think through life together from its very foundations and to attempt to find more things in common. Otherwise, the relationship runs the risk of drifting apart.

Nine of Pentacles

In general: Satisfaction arises from what you have achieved in life. There is a great deal of pride in success. This also enriches a relationship. Life is enjoyed to its fullest, and happiness is felt all around. There is harmonious agreement with the partner and the sharing of a lot of common interests.

    In a solid relationship: The relationship or the marriage stands on a solid foundation. You have arranged life in the way you imagined it. Despite harmonious togetherness, you both retain a certain measure of independence, pursuing and achieving your goals. You have substantially contributed to the success of this relationship without losing your own identity.

71

Nine of Pentacles Reversed

In general: A new relationship has not been realized despite a great deal of effort and loving dedication. Now you need to let go and not importune your partner any further, since this could, and with good reason, very quickly be read as obtrusiveness and molestation. Each person has the right to make his/her own choice. This disappointment can be filed under the category "experience."

Sometimes a person is in love and this love is not returned, no matter how much of an effort is made. The Nine of Pentacles Reversed asks you to let go and not to become importunate, even if that is hard. You will be enriched by the experience and will do better next time.

In a solid relationship: Something is not quite right in this seemingly perfect relationship or in this family, yet no one knows what precisely it is. Are you perhaps mimicking a successful couple, or are you deceiving yourselves? Have the problems been ignored for too long? Perhaps a hectic schedule of social obligations has left its traces and you find out at this point that you don't know each other as well as you previously believed, or you may have lost sight of each other. Professional and social success have become more important than the relationship, which has been pushed into the background. It would be a good idea to attempt at least once more to take a little more time for one another.

Ten of Pentacles

In general: You are fascinated by this new relationship and firmly believe you have found the partner for life this time. You think, feel, dream, and see only this human being and nothing else. There is the will to do everything possible in order to make this dream come true—even the readiness to legalize life together—that is, to get married. At one time you might not have considered it possible to be so conventional, but it has become a personal concern to officially stand by your partner.

In a solid relationship: You have succeeded professionally, and have both feet firmly planted on the ground. Social life is multi-faceted, and you may be a good host, if the situation calls for it. Attention and care are dedicated to the family and its needs. You are financially secure and do not have to worry about the future. The relationship or marriage stands on a solid foundation, based on mutual love and respect.

Ten of Pentacles Reversed

In general: Your partner would like to get married, but you have not shared this desire and are determined to put off the decision. In this way, you hope to gain time so as to come to terms with yourself before giving your partner a final answer. You are not ready for marriage yet.

In a solid relationship: You feel worn out between duties and tasks within the family. It is as if your identity has been lost. Your own wishes have been swallowed up by the needs and requests of the family; your personal dreams have been given up at least temporarily, though there is still some hope of having them fulfilled one day. You love your family and enjoy living in a sense of togetherness, but some needs and desires have become lost.

Even if you have always refused to legalize the relationship, it is now becoming serious. The Ten of Pentacles symbolizes the readiness to give in to the conventions in order to show the partner how much he/she is loved.

The Court Cards

The Court Cards are our companions in this dance of relationships. They represent the people we are dealing with and the qualities they possess. Keep in mind that the Pages, Knights, and Kings do not represent only men; the characteristics that are assigned to them can also be true for women. Conversely, Queens do not invariably represent women, but may also mirror the characteristics of men. When you place the cards and ask, for example, "How do I see my boyfriend?" it might very well be that for you—the Questioner—your boyfriend possesses the characteristics of a Queen.

The Court Cards show the characteristics and qualities of the people that surround us and play a role in our lives. At the same time, they reveal our own characteristics, and also, depending upon the question, how we are developing.

General Meanings of the Court Cards

Pages usually represent very young men or people who have never truly grown up—people who have held onto a youthful curiosity about life. Knights stand for people aged about 20 to 35 years old. The qualities assigned to the Knights, however, may be applied to people of, for example, 60 years of age, if they have preserved in themselves a certain elan and zest for life.

The Court Cards may describe you yourself as the Questioner, or they may answer questions that have been posed by other people. In one reading, more than one Court Card may appear that describes one and the same individual. When this happens, it may mean that the character traits of the person have changed in connection with the question. Through their association with Cups, Swords, Wands, or Pentacles, Court Cards also carry their own fundamental character traits. Cup-People, for example, are more sensitive than Sword-People, who tend to make decisions with the head. Wand-People make decisions spontaneously, while Pentacle-People never lose sight of the practical side of things.

74

The Cups

The Page of Cups

He dreams of love for the sake of love, though for him it shall still be lived and experienced from a distance, for he is not yet truly mature enough for a meaningful relationship. The Page of Cups is something of a troubadour, one of those who dream of romantic love and praise it without ever really wishing it to be fulfilled. He still has true feelings of love ahead of him. Although he already bears the Cup of Love in his hand, he has not yet devoted himself to the emotions that are linked with it. He prefers dreaming of his Ideal. Be cautious about getting involved with a Page, since he is still doing his apprenticeship in Love.

PAGE of CUPS.

The Page of Cups Reversed

The Page of Cups has become entangled in his dreams, and he can no longer find his way out. It is difficult for him to separate reality from his wishes and imaginings. He lives in a land of fantasy, intrigued with what appears unattainable, but he knows precisely what he wants. He will strive to manipulate the feelings of others in order to get it.

The Knight of Cups

He has left the stage of dreams behind and has moved his idea of Love into reality. Always in search of the ideal love, he embodies the wish of many women who dream of the knight on the white steed who carries them off to the land of eternal love and passion. He is charming, attractive, and irresistible to many. His charm is eluded only with great difficulty. Who knows, perhaps someone can tame him—it might be worth a try. Yet the Knight of Cups is an idealist; he loves Love and Feelings, but he is not prepared to attach himself to a

KNIGHT of CUPS.

75

partner. He is on his way through, always in search of the ever more beautiful, more tempting feeling of love, and the feeling of being in love. He stands before the river of emotions, but he does not cross it for, though so close, he does not wish to yield to this reality.

The Knight of Cups Reversed would like to avoid all responsibilities and will evade any obligation. If you let yourself be beguiled by his charms, you are playing with fire.

The Knight of Cups Reversed

What has just been said about the Knight of Cups moves into negative realms when the card is reversed. He uses his charms and his appeal for the emotional manipulation of the people in his surroundings. He knows how one to play with people's emotions and does it—to his advantage and without scruple. He avoids any responsibility, and manages to take advantage of people through his charming behavior and appealing manners. The highest caution is advised in dealing with this Knight of Cups.

QUEEN of CUPS.

The Queen of Cups

She is an emotional woman. Her kingdom lies in the world of feelings, and thus she thinks and behaves completely emotionally as well. She sits very close to the Waters of Emotion with which she thoroughly identifies herself. This means that she is dreamy, loves with considerable drama, and only acts according to her feelings. She is ready to live for love and to give everything to a relationship. Often unselfish and sometimes naïve, she gladly helps others, which is often reflected in her social involvement. She is creative. Her happiness does not so much depend upon material things, but rather upon her personal fulfillment. As an idealist, she is always on the search for Beauty. A woman of intuition, she prefers to linger in nature to refresh her power, to relax, and to get the necessary rest for her soul.

The Queen of Cups Reversed

The emotional qualities change into a chaos of feelings. She has become entangled in them. Whining and self-pitying, she refuses to accept the realities of life. Instead, she yields to diffuse dreams of love and an untouched world. This is a dangerous way to live, because the sense of reality can easily be lost. You can't rely on the Queen of Cups Reversed, since she seems to live on another planet.

The King of Cups

He is the man who brings help; he is sensitive and a very attractive person. Feelings surge around him, yet he himself remains reserved despite his readiness to help. You often find him in a social career, yet he keeps his own feelings private; he seems unavailable. Perhaps he is afraid of his own feelings and lives in the belief that he will be overcome by them if he expresses them. So he has created a distance. He is as the water in a desert mirage, so near, and yet unattainable.

KING of CUPS.

The King of Cups Reversed

Here again, every moral consideration is thrown overboard. The King of Cups Reversed is dishonest and possessive. He knows instinctively how to manipulate his surroundings, and shamelessly uses this knowledge for his own purposes. It is very likely that he has lost interest in his relationship. If he stays, it is probably because he sees it as comfortable; his partner is there to make his life as pleasant as possible. He knows how to look after his own interests and conveniences, and he understands as well how to use words or make confessions of love that bring him closer to his goals.

The King of Cups is charming and helpful, but otherwise unapproachable. He uses his helpfulness as a veil, behind which he conceals his feelings. He will open up to very few people.

The Swords

The Page of Swords

PAGE of SWORDS.

The Page of Swords is curious about life and often plays crazy pranks. He also takes great pleasure in lively arguments. He finds it wonderful when he wins a discussion, but he is also open to counterargument, if his opponents possess the persistence needed to convince him they are right. With him, almost everything runs through the intellect—he loves to exercise his mind in one way or another—and with his intelligence, he often hits the nail on the head. He gladly fades out, however, in the area of the emotions.

Full of determination, he knows what he wants. Everything that has to do with communication interests this Page. He tries out many new things, and loves to take advantage of life and all its possibilities. As a partner, he can be rather trying, since you feel as if you always have to be on guard about what you say, because he quickly turns your words around. You can experience a lot with him and, at his side, make the most of the pleasures of life. But a solid relationship is not for him; he would like to see more of the world before he commits himself.

The Page of Swords gladly plays with his wits. He loves word games and discussions—the livelier, the better. He wants to know who is quickest and makes the best arguments. He is not a suitable partner for peace-lovers.

The Page of Swords Reversed

This Page knows very well that he can, with his sharp intellect, easily hurt others and create uncertainty, and he is only too happy to do that. His manipulations are direct: he may conceal his own anxieties or desires by sowing suspicions that create uncertainty in his partner, in an effort to bind her more to him, make her more dependent on him, or even to have some sly fun with her. The Page of Swords Reversed loves to stir up doubts and enjoys spreading gossip. It is best to be cautious with the reversed Page of Swords, as he stops his little games neither for his family nor his friends, when it is in his interests. Do not believe everything that is served up here, and scrutinize his motives and actions very carefully.

The Knight of Swords

KNIGHT of SWORDS.

The Knight of Swords is as changeable as the clouds through which he rushes on the card illustration. Today he is a passionate lover; tomorrow, he turns cold and aloof. Through his moodiness, he brings unrest and excitement into life. He knows what he wants, and he knows where he wants to go. Will he include his partner in his plans? He usually does not know yet, for the Knight of Swords loves his freedom. He makes sudden, unexpected decisions. He brings fun and change, for he cannot tolerate boredom. Spiritually, he is flighty, always on the search for something new. Taking responsibility in the long run or committing himself pleases him less, because he fears being locked in or constricted through a close relationship. If you enter a relationship with such a Knight, be aware that he can, most likely, only be held on a very long leash.

The Knight of Swords approaches like a windstorm. Today, he is passionate; tomorrow, he is distant. He knows what he wants. Whether he will include a partner in his plans is his secret.

The Knight of Swords Reversed

This Knight can be very destructive. Only his will matters, which he must push through at any price. He does not shrink from meanness and underhanded plans, and perhaps even finds it amusing when he reaches his goal through them. Watch out for him, for he can appear very attractive through his determination and brashness, especially to those who have difficulty standing up for themselves. He will not stop for anyone, for he wants to assert his will.

The Queen of Swords

The Queen of Swords knows what she wants. Her reason

QUEEN of SWORDS.

rules her heart, and she loves to stake the sharpness of her intellect against that of others. Such a woman must be given the chance to measure herself in her relationship. She does not enjoy being limited or bound and, as a result, often avoids relationships. She has probably had a previous marriage, which was not the best experience. She loves her independence and freedom of thought, and she is not willing to have them taken away from her. She understands very well how to hold onto them—with keen perception and wit.

Yet if you were to break through the wall of her independence, undeterred by her sharp tongue, you would find a woman who is very loyal and helpful and upon whom you can rely. She searches continually for new spiritual challenges. If she has lost interest, whether in the relationship or in other things, then nothing will and no one can change her mind. It is not easy to conquer or to keep the love of a Queen of Swords, but it might be fun to try.

The Queen of Swords Reversed

The Queen of Swords Reversed has surrendered herself to self-pity. For her, everyone else is to blame, only she is free of guilt. She does not want to see that she bears responsibility for her own life. Thus, she lives on in her self-pity, refusing to see it, keeping such a self-portrait far away.

She has wrapped herself in a coat of loneliness and is now very solitary. She cannot be persuaded that she herself has contributed to her sorrow through her unapproachability or that she expects too much from the people around her. She is disappointed when her overly high expectations are not fulfilled, which confirms her opinion that only she can do things correctly. She is a perfectionist and expects perfection from other people. With this behavior she drives away a lot of people whom she may have considered very decent. So she quarrels with her fate and finds no way out of the labyrinth of self-pity that she has constructed for herself. You've got to feel sorry for her, but she cannot stand sympathy; to this she reacts indignantly.

The King of Swords

He is a sharp-witted man who conceals his emotions behind his intellect. He is helpful and a good organizer, but he faces feelings with wariness, navigating life with his head. He loves stimulating conversation and good entertainment. He can be your best friend or worst enemy; he does nothing half-heartedly. A professional, he prefers self-reliance to dependence, for he relies little upon what others say and prefers to come to his own conclusions. If he grants his help, he does so with circumspection and reason. You can rely on him in any situation. However, he does not want to be told what to do in a relationship. A prudent companion, he sees his relationship as the interplay of mutual support. He would like a just or fair distribution of responsibility, to have each role fulfilled. He is conscientious but, with his sharp tongue, he can seem offensive at times.

KING of SWORDS.

He does not allow others to look into his business without a fuss, for he keeps his thoughts to himself until he has determined just what they are and is ready to express them. He must prove his inner independence and his freedom of decision again and again, otherwise he feels constricted. Living with a King of Swords is not always easy.

The King of Swords Reversed

The King of Swords has lost all trustworthiness. He has turned into a tyrannical and despotic ruler. Everything must revolve around him. He is ruthless and can also become violent in order to carry out his will. Moreover, he is capricious and undependable: you cannot rely upon his word. He uses his intellect to hurt people and to press his advantage at any price. It would be wise to approach this King of Swords with suspicion, for he knows how to make your life unbearable.

The Wands

The Page of Wands

PAGE of WANDS.

The Page of Wands is creative, jolly, and always in the mood for a joke. When you're with him, you're always in good company. He has a vivacious spirit and is rather restless and volatile. He knows that life has a lot to offer, and would like to have a relationship on a rather casual basis—not too close or intense. His desire for freedom is far greater than his desire to be attached. However, he is not dishonest, nor does he try to take advantage of his partner. He merely has an insatiable curiosity about new things, ideas, and people, which he may find around the next corner and which he has not yet explored. If you get involved with this Page, you can look forward to an interesting and hot love. Don't try, however, to nail him down; better to wait until he himself is ready and then seize the initiative.

The Page of Wands Reversed

Here the Page of Wands is very superficial, one who follows only his own pleasure. Although he promises a lot, he follows through on very little, and then only if it suits him. Carefully weigh the statements of this Page, for he is not to be trusted. He is a joker who happily enjoys himself to the detriment of others.

The Knight of Wands

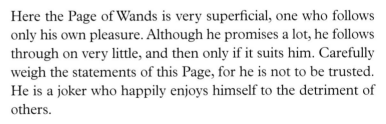

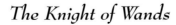

KNIGHT of WANDS.

The Knight of Wands is a charmer. He loves life, is witty, lively, and full of ideas. He can not tolerate boredom, but searches continually for new creative challenges. He loves love, but not responsibility, and possesses great appeal for the opposite sex. The first to know what the "in thing" is, he belongs to the type of up-and-coming young businessman or entrepreneur (this of course can apply to women as well), who is always busy doing something. For him, life is a challenge that must be accepted. Relationships are part of his lifestyle; they are, however, more of a bonus than a staple of life. And yet you will be prepared to forgive him almost anything.

The Knight of Wands Reversed

He is someone who knows only his own ambitions, and to achieve them, he will step over bodies, if it becomes necessary. His advantage is the sole criterion that counts in his life. He will do almost anything to further his interests, even if others must fall by the wayside. Only become involved with this Knight of Wands with a great deal of caution. He will pretend to be in love, but his only intentions are his advantage and comfort. He spreads his charm around in order to get his victims where he wants them. He will drop his partner without any warning if she no longer fits in with his plans.

The Queen of Wands

Creativity and curiosity about life with all of its challenges are characteristic of the Queen of Wands. She is charming and helpful, and she provides loyalty and assistance to her partner.

The Queen of Wands is warm-hearted with a great deal of eroticism. She usually has a quick intellect and is engaged in spiritual ideas. She can translate her dreams and ideas into action. Her partner is provided assistance and loyalty, as long as he doesn't try to put her in a cage. Should you constrict her too much, she will lose the charm that is so fascinating.

QUEEN of WANDS.

She gives good advice and, if asked, is always ready to help and envision herself in her partner's situation. However, she does not like boredom and busies herself with new and exciting ideas. She is independent and manages well the division between the fulfillment of her desires and her duties in regard to her family, if she has one.

The Queen of Wands Reversed

She is afraid of her own independence and strives to conceal her uncertainty beneath grand gestures, behind showy appearances. In addition, she enjoys getting involved in matters that do not concern her. As a partner, she is possessive, demanding, and unforgiving. She likes to be the center of attention, and will use any means possible to do so.

The King of Wands

KING of WANDS.

He is successful in his career, helpful, and creative. In a relationship, he will bring you pleasant thrills: he might, for example, quite spontaneously invite you out for an evening of theatre or an elegant dinner for two. In his society, you feel very comfortable due to his immense charm. In his career, he knows what he wants, and loves a challenge. He can also be a strain, however, because he demands the same degree of enthusiasm from the people around him that he himself brings. He does not forget, at any time, his responsibilities toward his family.

He enjoys providing service to others. He may be working with an honorary association or a charitable organization; but in any case he will work where he is able to realize his creative talents. As a partner, you need to grant freedom to such a King; he needs it for his development.

The King of Wands Reversed demands that his partner subordinate herself to him unconditionally. Such an egotistical attitude brings no true love or happiness for either partner.

The King of Wands Reversed

He is ambitious, self-centered, and inconsiderate. He demands that his partner subordinate herself to him unconditionally; otherwise, he becomes furious and can quickly lose control. As a partner, he is very difficult, because he accepts only his own opinions and will not even listen to others. Though he is adverse to intentionally provoking fights and conflicts, he uses his charm wherever it can be used for his advantage.

84

The Pentacles

The Page of Pentacles

The Page of Pentacles is practical: he prefers occupying himself with things that he can touch rather than with abstractions, and he has no head for theory. What matters for him is the solid, the concrete—what one can taste, feel, or touch. He is reliable, but slightly uncertain in his intentions. To be sure, he knows what he wants and is also prepared to work for his goals, yet he still lacks sufficient experience. He is shy rather than outgoing, but friendly and helpful. In a relationship, he is restrained and cautious, because he does not want to promise anything that he cannot fulfill. Above all, he would like to be very certain before he commits to a confining relationship. He handles money carefully, and has already planned his financial future.

PAGE of PENTACLES.

The Page of Pentacles Reversed

If you ask something of this Page of Pentacles, he may promise, but he will not stick to it. He does as he pleases. If you find no place in his life, his feeling is that it's your tough luck. He is unreliable and foolish with regard to financial matters. Narrow-minded, possessive, and rather lazy, he loves to order around the people close to him and have them dance to his whistle.

The Knight of Pentacles

The Knight of Pentacles is always ready to help. He is hard-working and not too proud to help with household chores. He lacks a touch of creativity, an easy-going nature, spontaneity, the ability to decide things off the top of his head; these are not possible for him. However, you can count on him, and he will hold to his word. He appears to possess

The Knight of Pentacles is a calm and helpful person, who fulfills his duties conscientiously. He may not be the most thrilling of partners, but he embodies the character traits of patience, perseverance, and reliability.

85

inexhaustible patience. Extremely precise in money matters, he approaches all things of life with great prudence. He may perhaps never be the boss of a firm, for he lacks the capacity for great leadership, but he is well-respected for his industry and his flexibility in his professional as well as in his private life.

The Knight of Pentacles Reversed

This Knight is extremely narrow-minded and has tremendous egoism. It is his opinion alone that counts. He stands in opposition to every innovation with iron determination, for his motto is "If it was good enough before, then it is good enough now." Lacking foresight and flexibility, he is impatient and despotic; he forces his opinions on his partner and accepts nothing else. With such a partner, a fight always erupts regarding money, for he shirks his responsibilities and prefers to let the other person pay. He is as stingy as he is intolerant.

The Queen of Pentacles

The Queen of Pentacles is a warm-hearted and helpful woman. She has turned toward the concrete side of life and likes to know where she stands in a relationship. Uncertain situations may cause her trouble. If she gets involved in a stable relationship, she does so with a great deal of thought. For her, practical considerations, in addition to feelings, are what make a relationship successful, such as, financial security, a place to live, or similar things. She does not give herself away easily and spontaneously. Since material matters are important to her, she is ready to work hard for her goals. She loves the fine things in life, but spends little time dreaming of them. A conservative and reliable partner, she will rise to the challenge of her tasks, be they family or work or both, when circumstances require it, and she will risk everything in order to make her wishes come true.

The Queen of Pentacles Reversed

For this Queen, only money counts. She prefers to choose her partner for his career opportunities and his income rather than for other values. She would like to have, if possible, all the things that her heart desires. The partner comes off second best. Her interests, above all in material things, are for her so important that she is even prepared to put up with an inconvenient relationship. She can be very extravagant, and set her interests before anything else. If she wants to achieve her desires and goals, she can be cold and inconsiderate, or, on the other hand, sometimes enticing. It is not pleasant living with this Queen if you oppose her desires.

The King of Pentacles

This King has achieved something in his life: he stands solidly with two feet on the ground of facts, and finds his way well within reality. He knows what he wants, and plans prudently where he will go on the path of life. Financially, he is secure. He is not one to experiment with changeable relationships, but acts rather calmly and reservedly, as he does in other matters. The King of Pentacles often comes across as a rather conservative person; for him, family and work come first. Thanks to his helpful nature and his practical knowledge, people often ask him for assistance.

The King of Pentacles Reversed

Here, the King is weak and ineffective. He has dropped the reins and given his partner a free hand. He would like to be left in peace and to assume as little responsibility as possible. The fine arts are lost labors of love for this King. He prefers spending his time in front of the television set or with the boys. The desires of his partner are of no consequence to him.

The Queen of Pentacles Reversed loves money. For her, economic security comes before all else, and she will act accordingly, using every means to bring her closer to her goal. If you enter into a relationship with her, you hopefully have enough money in your pocket; otherwise she will not stay around long.

QUEEN of PENTACLES.

The Major Arcana

The Major Arcana describes our inner life, how we feel, think, or cope, what motivates us. These cards show us whether we need to change something in our thinking in order to enter into a happy, fulfilling relationship.

The Major Arcana reflects our inner life. It shows us what we think and feel, what we fear, and even what drives us. Our innermost desire is the driving force of our actions. Our yearning for a new love compels us to go in search of it. The cards of the Major Arcana tell us how we regard a relationship, whether we are optimistic about it or negative. Perhaps we are afraid of a new relationship, though we declare that we wish for nothing more passionately. Or perhaps we have protected within ourselves that curiosity for life and are prepared to take a new path in love as well.

0 The Fool

Here is the chance to dare a new beginning, with no idea where it will lead. The Fool is the impulse that drives us to be interested in one another and to risk the adventure of a relationship. The entire world has turned upside down all of a sudden, and you are ready to jump symbolically off the edge, to open up to both joy and sorrow with the challenges of a new relationship. This readiness cannot be explained with reason, for it comes from inner feelings and is irresistible. The everyday ordered world is drastically different, yet no one is startled by this condition.

THE FOOL.

What you have to deal with is uncertain, and it is not possible to know how it will turn out. A sign from heaven has provided a bit of luck, and you are strongly determined to seize this chance. Any well-intentioned advice is ignored. The Fool relies on his intuition and his new-found sense of adventure. There is no guarantee of the success of the relationship; however, there is a chance, which the Fool is counting on. Perhaps you are plunging into the adventure of parenthood and are prepared to give your life new meaning through children. You may encounter the unexpected.

0 The Fool Reversed

Fear of the step into uncertainty makes its presence known, for you would like to be guaranteed that this decision is worth it, emotionally or financially. You don't yet feel ready to open the door to the unexpected and try the adventure of a relationship and partnered life. You see only the problems that could come about and not the possible joys. It is difficult to realize dreams, if you don't have the courage to do something spontaneous at least once. You fear leaving behind the old and familiar. A relationship comes to nothing.

I The Magician

THE MAGICIAN.

The Magician brings together every symbol of the Tarot, and through them demonstrates confidence in his own power, the dynamic force that carries him toward his goal. The Magician is a signpost, the inner voice that establishes the bridge from the conscious to the unconscious. He can function as an advisor, if the person listens inside and pays attention to dreams; he explains that you can have self-assurance and be full of confidence about a relationship. The Magician also represents a strong, positive partner who can be relied upon.

In a new relationship, goals are reached through perseverance and personal conviction. Don't let yourself be discouraged if what you strive for is not achieved immediately. It is this confidence that exemplifies what the Magician offers. Things will take a turn for the better.

The Magician demands deliberate positive action. In regard to relationships, he knows that happiness can be greatly helped along if you are determined to seize the initiative. Never forget that your own thoughts are the beginning of any action. The Magician symbolizes those positive thoughts that open previously undreamed-of possibilities. Therefore, the answer is not waiting and brooding, but rather translating confident desires into action.

The Magician says that hesitation and self-doubt are not reasonable. You should and can have confidence in yourself and in your partner. Positive thinking is the great mark of the Magician.

I The Magician Reversed

Self-confidence has changed to uncertainty. The Magician has become a weak partner on whom the other cannot rely. Ambitious plans are never realized. This is a person who does not want to have his/her plans known and prefers leaving his partner in the dark, be it about money or the relationship.

In a new relationship, confidence has been abandoned and you are left with only the hope that next time will be easier. It's important to pinpoint the source of this uncertainty, so that it can be overcome. Negative thoughts, the reflected images of our inner selves, bring negative results.

The High Priestess symbolizes your unconscious. She confirms your sensitivity, intuition, and empathy. Make use of these qualities and trust in your inner voice.

II The High Priestess

Just as the Magician represents the conscious, so the High Priestess shows us the unconscious. She possesses sensitivity, intuition, and empathy. She speaks of the serious side of life and gets little pleasure from superficiality.

In a relationship, this card means that you know yourself very well, and also know intuitively what your partner thinks, feels, or wants to say. It is as if you are a great team and don't need a lot of words in order to understand each other. A soul-kinship binds you together. Through this close attachment, you are each ready to fulfill the other's wishes, whenever possible. This bond is likely to become ever more profound, and the two of you will be able to communicate on deep subjects, such as the meaning of life and the world of the unconscious.

As a new relationship, this connection can really bowl you over. There is the unbelievable feeling that you have already known each other for years, and a very unusual intimacy, though you do not know anything very much about each other yet.

THE HIGH PRIESTESS.

II *The High Priestess Reversed*

Be careful that your connection to reality is not lost. You have become so entangled in the fascinating world of dreams that you would like to forget that reality with all its joys and necessities even exists. A relationship is experienced like a dream, in which you are grateful not to feel alone. Your partner, on the other hand, may not be at all aware of this. We cannot evade the reality of life; when we do, loneliness is the end result. In a new relationship, the couple talks past each other, for each is so occupied with his/her own business that they are not prepared to deal with the problems of the partner. They are not unaware, however, of the feelings of the other. If this relationship is to function, a change in perspective is necessary; for example, they might be prepared to truly listen and show genuine understanding.

The High Priestess Reversed has taken refuge in a world of illusion, and it is difficult for her to distinguish between the illusion and reality. So she lives for the day and avoids difficulties, if possible.

III *The Empress*

The Empress embodies the maternal principle in its most beautiful form. Without the readiness to bring something about with patience, to nourish it, to look after it, and to see it grow, our world can not prosper. Here the Empress sits in the middle of a fruitful landscape, which symbolizes growth. She radiates calm and composure and trusts in her inner strength, which comes to her aid. She is careful and helpful, the calming center of a relationship, full of ideas for the shaping of a more beautiful life together. She is ready to take care of the well-being of her family, and not only physically. A happy, harmonious family life lets everyone involved draw power for everyday existence. This card can also symbolize marriage or pregnancy.

THE EMPRESS.

With a new relationship, it is important for her to find a person who knows how to appreciate the helpfulness and warmth of family life. Someone with too great a need for freedom would only make this Empress unhappy.

III The Empress Reversed

Where the Empress is patient and careful, the Empress Reversed suffocates any sense of togetherness through patronizing and egoism. A partner in this situation does not enjoy staying home.

Instead of supporting the partner, the Empress Reversed tries to dictate what the person should do and won't let him/her forgot what she has already done for him/her. Egoism has free rein. The partner is instructed to act according to the Empress's own ideas, and she takes every occasion to dominate the partner's opinions, thereby suffocating any sense of togetherness. The partner subsequently would rather stay away from home than be in that unfriendly atmosphere. In a new relationship, she runs the partner over with her own desires and selfish ideas. Such behavior promises no great success.

IV The Emperor

The Emperor embodies a sense of responsibility connected with the readiness to assume responsibility. The goals he has set for himself are also realized. With theories, he can do little. Under the symbol of the Emperor, plans are translated into action. In a relationship, he is the strong shoulder on which his partner can lean.

THE EMPEROR.

In a family, he is a committed father, who is concerned about the well-being of his loved ones and tries to act strictly but also with benevolence. He has a great deal of understanding of his partner, and also takes the necessary time after work to calmly deal with the worries and needs of other family members. In a new relationship, the Emperor represents a love on which you can depend. Here no empty promises are given, but instead a meaningful declaration of love from the heart. The Emperor represents a man who knows what he wants and is prepared to commit himself to his ideals. Carelessness does not suit him. If you get to know such a man, you are in good hands with well-intentioned thoughtfulness and love.

IV The Emperor Reversed

One of the partners is very dominant and always wants the last word. Hence, the relationship becomes very unpleasant and difficult. The Emperor Reversed has become the house-tyrant, who accepts only his own opinion. He expects that all the family members will be obedient, as the desires of the partner or the children are of little consequence. What is important is that his own goals are taken into consideration and fulfilled. The power he enjoys is generally received at the expense of the family. He may not shrink from violence either. It is very unhealthy in a relationship when one partner acts as a tyrant.

In a new relationship, The Emperor Reversed frightens the other away through this self-interested behavior.

He heads the house as an absolute dictator and also feels like one. The Emperor Reversed has marked out his realm in which everyone has to obey. Such high-handedness does not make for a happy relationship, so a change in attitude is necessary.

V The Hierophant

The Hierophant symbolizes the counselor. His insight and well-thought-out advice comes from conventional sources as well as from the spiritual side of life. He gives advice and comfort, expects loyalty from people around him, and is prepared to give this loyalty right back. Completely taken up in his responsibilities, he sees in them the meaning of his life. He enjoys passing along his earned insights, if asked, and is always by anybody's side with word and deed. If he has committed to a relationship, then the Hierophant prefers a traditional arrangement, for he does not like doing things by halves. He translates his promises of a great love into action.

THE HIEROPHANT.

This card can also indicate an engagement or a wedding to take place sometime soon.

V The Hierophant Reversed

If this card appears, the person always knows better than other people. The person gives advice, even when it is not asked for, and expects everybody to stand amazed by this

THE LOVERS.

wisdom. He/she talks too much, does not listen to others, and is of the firm opinion that he knows precisely what is good for the partner and also for the family. Taking the slight trouble to listen to the partner once in a while would certainly be worth the effort. Perhaps the person would learn to get to know his partner, who by now may be resigned to his/her fate through silence and being disregarded or told what to do.

In a young relationship, the Hierophant Reversed makes decisions without consulting the partner. It would make a great deal of sense to inquire about the wishes of the partner, especially if there is a desire for the relationship to continue.

VI The Lovers

If you are hoping that love will finally run smoothly, your moment has come. The card of the Lovers is the card of right decisions—a confirmation of whatever you have made up your mind to do, be it to risk starting on a new love, spend your first night together, or embark on a more solid relationship.

This is the right moment for a new love. If you have been full of doubt, this card will confirm that you are acting wisely. Happiness will be fulfilled.

In a relationship, you feel loved and protected. There is great understanding and consideration between the partners. The intimacy is deep, and each feels that the partner has been known for a long time. At least one of them wishes to delight the other with little surprises, and enjoys it when this happiness is reflected in the face of the other. In a new love, they may be convinced that the ideal partner has been pursued and found. The card of the Lovers indicates that they believe they have arrived at their goal in matters of the heart.

VI The Lovers Reversed

Filled with the feelings of being in love, you may be so overpowered that you cannot or do not want to face the fact that you are being exploited. Your partner may be speaking with an angelic tongue to get what he/she wants, and will not shy away from using sex as a means to an end. You may be discriminated against in this relationship. An inner distance is necessary in order to be able to analyze objectively your life together.

If this is a new relationship and there have been plans to move in together, it would be a good idea to put the project on ice for now. The moment for that has not yet arrived. Although love makes a person blind, it would be advisable to examine this relationship for a good while to determine whether you want to go into a shared endeavor and whether you can really vouch for your partner. Think very seriously about it from a safe distance; not everything is as it appears.

VII The Chariot

THE CHARIOT.

The Chariot represents the contrasts in a relationship, which you can bring into a harmonious whole. Sometimes you may have to fight for the partner and this card shows that it will be worth it.

Perhaps the partners have been drifting apart, yet suddenly togetherness and community have become important once more. The Chariot Driver recognizes what he has in his partner and admits to mistakes made in the past. Perhaps he has plunged into work so much that the shared life has been pushed into the background. He may have let the reins drag, but now he is ready to make some serious compromises in order to save the partnership. While it may be possible to restructure the relationship, it is possible that the partner will not want to commit to it without further thought. Perhaps too many promises were given in the past that were not kept. The Chariot Driver must realize that the desires of the partner must be considered as well as his own. Perhaps the old feelings have gotten lost in the hectic activity of everyday life, through the responsibilities of the family, or through his own egotistical wants.

In a new relationship, things will be talked over and the partners will manage to clearly define the wishes and hopes

The Chariot shows the readiness to change something. If a person has been acting in a domineering fashion, he/she has now become reasonable and ready to change this behavior. The relationship has again moved into the foreground.

for this relationship. They are ready to compromise without having the feeling that anything is being given up.

VII The Chariot Reversed

The only things that are important to the Chariot Reversed are his/her desires and their fulfillment. Whether or not this pleases the partner plays absolutely no role—only those interests count. Then it is a great surprise when relationships do not last so long or the marriage has become loveless. Any personal failures are shifted over onto the other person. If the relationship is to be maintained, then this behavior needs to be rethought, the partner's needs looked after, and the respective desires and expectations addressed.

Strength symbolizes the mental power and inner balance that you have earned after weathering the strokes of fate time and again. Insight and tolerance have set in.

VIII Strength

Mental maturity and insight have been achieved; the strokes of fate have been mastered, and you have emerged stronger. Life may have been very difficult, demanding a lot of vigor and strong nerves. Perhaps there was an illness in the family, or you had to bear all the responsibility of childcare as a single parent. Now you are again in a position to devote yourself seriously to a new relationship.

In an already existing relationship, mutual problems have been overcome together. These can be of the financial or family kind. For this, the partners had to fall back upon their personal inner reserves.

Some people have things come to them very easily, while others must struggle very hard. Defiance of fate is the path to understanding and to tolerance.

STRENGTH.

VIII Strength Reversed

You have surrendered to unrestrained self-pity and find it secretly pleasurable, even if you deny it on the outside. At last, you can tell others how terribly it is going. Perhaps you are even taking pills in order to deal with all kinds of different boo-boos. Having to take medicine proves how much you are suffering.

Possibly, a relationship has come to an end, or else the partner has become oriented elsewhere, for no one can endure so much self-pity and the resulting accusations and suspicions for long. You have managed what you set out to accomplish: you can now wrangle with fate alone. However, we are the masters of our destinies and have chosen our own ways. If you wish to lead a fulfilling life, then you need to seek a way out of this depression. As the old saying goes: "Laugh and the world laughs with you, cry and you cry alone."

IX *The Hermit*

THE HERMIT.

The Hermit symbolizes inner seclusion. You are occupied a great deal with your own thoughts and prefer to live in solitude. This manner of living is natural, for you need this loneliness in order to think peacefully about the self and the world. This seclusion is not seen as loneliness.

In a relationship, you can keep the companion at a distance through this attitude, or he/she may feel locked out. Perhaps you are one who makes all the decisions without including the partner. While you may always have the well-being of the partner clearly in mind, that person's opinion is not asked. It is very likely that the partner will feel offended by this exclusionary behavior. With such an imbalance in the relationship, the partners can quickly become isolated. So it's important for you to try hard to become more open.

At times the Hermit knows that something is not right in the relationship, because a quiet inner warning voice keeps saying to pay more attention. It is not necessarily true that the relationship is unhappy or endangered, but it is lacking the expression of true unity. As the Hermit, you may find yourself confronted with a not very clearly defined danger to the relationship. It is important to pay more attention to that

People who are very introverted prefer to think things over for themselves before they ask the partner or give an answer. This behavior is symbolized by the Hermit.

inner voice, for many beautiful shared moments can otherwise be lost. The Hermit can also represent the inner advisor who stands at your side.

IX The Hermit Reversed

To take advice or to listen to other warnings of danger is nothing to the Hermit Reversed. His calm and comfort extends to include everything. The relationship is characterized by boredom.

As the Hermit Reversed, you are not willing to solve problems by discussing them. You never listen to advice; this is for other people to do. You consider that the relationship is very well-maintained, things are apparently going well for your partner and, as for the rest, you'll take life as it comes. You feel it's enough for the two of you to live somewhat reasonably side by side—but not necessary to be exciting partners. Great silences or excruciating boredom often rule. Television may be the best friend, if through it, the Hermit can hide. You are full of mistrust in regard to each and every thing and would like only to be left alone to enjoy the well-deserved calm. How does it look to the partner—does he/she agree? Oh well, who knows? Nobody's asking!

X The Wheel of Fortune

WHEEL of FORTUNE.

New hope prevails, for order has been brought back into life, which is free from inner conflict and negative thoughts. Life is taken as a challenge. Solitude has come to an end, and you are once more looking toward a beautiful life as a couple.

In a relationship, you have overcome turbulent times; you may even have arrived at the realization that life and love cannot exist only as fun, but that you must also take on the responsibilities of a harmonious life together. If you have struggled with financial difficulties, an improvement is now in sight. Professional problems that have burdened the relationship are resolved, or that perfect apartment, the one that you have always sought, is finally found. You are looking toward the shared future with great confidence. The Wheel of Fortune has turned and you are on the way up.

X The Wheel of Fortune Reversed

If you brace yourself against every change in life, you will make your existence very difficult. Most people do not want to accept the fact that life changes constantly, and they seek to hold on with all their might to what is possessed and known. Your partner might possibly like to make alterations, but you know how to prevent this with all available resources. Perhaps it is a location or career change that you don't want to accept for fear of new challenges. But even if you want to hold onto the past with all your strength, the flow of life will not be stopped. Don't forget that an ending always holds in it the opportunity for a new beginning—and who can ever say that such a new beginning will not lead to even greater things? It would be well never to lose your curiosity about life.

It is always difficult in life to accept a change that is sometimes necessary for further development. If you fight this change tooth and nail, The Wheel of Fortune Reversed shows that you will make your life very difficult.

XI Justice

Justice symbolizes the cool reason of the logical thinker. Feelings are not expressed, for you are skeptical about strong emotion. In crisis situations, a balance is created between feelings and reason. In case of doubt, you feel that rationality should be the victor.

In a relationship, you probably act in an extremely rational manner, which the partner can only break through with a great show of feelings. But too many feelings can make you quite uncomfortable; you need a little distance. It's not that you're indifferent, but being led by reason, you are protected against the chaos of a decision made instinctively. And your fellow creatures agree with you, since you are often asked for help in untangling the bedlam that can arise from impulsive action.

You can bear responsibility and are able to live up to most challenges. A fair and objective partner, you can be relied upon in any circumstances.

99

XI Justice Reversed

Justice Reversed points to the idea that you have lost your perspective and passed over the consequences of your actions with little or no thought. This greatly burdens a relationship.

If this card turns up, you do not like to think logically, and, in addition, you believe that nothing is gained from long reflection anyway. If decisions come up in a more spontaneous manner, then you act on them immediately, and think about the consequences later. For the partner or for the family, this is very exciting, sometimes even wearying, as none of you are certain what will happen next. Many of these decisions may have turned out badly, as you have not taken enough time to think them through. Spontaneity is great, but sometimes you need to keep your limits in mind—in financial matters, for example. Perhaps the family is pulled into a lavish lifestyle that they truly do not want. You expect your partner to understand your actions, as well as, depending on the circumstances, your lack of responsibility.

XII The Hanged Man

THE HANGED MAN.

The Hanged Man symbolizes the readiness to sacrifice in order to attain something better and greater. If you live alone, the Hanged Man can mean that you are ready to withdraw and think over your attitude toward relationships, so that they can be ordered anew. This is sometimes a long and difficult process that calls for a great deal of soul-searching, and the truths that are uncovered are not always pleasant. The trouble is worth it, however, for you are in a position to change your perspective as well as your life. You have the opportunity to free yourself from old patterns of thought.

The Hanged Man means that everything is turned upside down. Relations that existed up to this point are put into a new order. If you were facing a separation, it may be that you can avert it now. If you are ready to rethink your attitude toward your partner, you may open up a new chance for a shared life. Sacrifices are demanded, an inner-and-outer transformation that will prove fortunate in the long run.

Perhaps there will be the loss of a job or some other sudden event; in any case, a complete change will take place. If your children have grown up, this card can symbolize their ever increasing independence, compelling you to fill the rising emptiness in a meaningful way.

In a new relationship, you are prepared to commit to the partner, even if it means a sacrifice. Perhaps you move in so that you can be close to the new partner, or perhaps you even change your occupation for the same reason. It might also mean that you fundamentally change your attitude towards the relationship. If you were formerly unwilling to be tied down, you may now be ready to commit yourself. Whatever the sacrifice, it is always made freely and gladly.

XII *The Hanged Man Reversed*

With this card, you consider yourself the eternal victim: you are not prepared to change your inner perspective about yourself and your environment, and as a result, you will attract the very same problems time and time again in your relationships. The problem lies within yourself and your own inflexible attitudes. In addition, you continually fall in love with the same type of partner who confirms your role as victim. You do not want to understand that a change in your perspective is necessary in order to attain a change in your relationships.

Of the opinion that you will never find happiness, you place the blame on someone else. In a relationship, you waste away from self-pity and lament that too much is demanded by the partner or by the family. With this attitude, you yourself are demanding a great deal of the family, as they must listen to your incessant complaints. Yet you can only create happiness through having a healthy perspective of yourself and other people. This calls for a journey inward and for the readiness to recognize that you often contribute a great deal to your problems.

The Hanged Man symbolizes sacrifice, but there is a positive willingness to make this sacrifice. You are prepared to rethink your life, look at it from a different perspective, and order it anew.

DEATH.

Death is one of the most positive cards of Tarot, for it promises a renewal, a rebirth. Self-confidence returns and a relationship that promises happiness and trust after an unhappy past, is to be expected. The future fulfills what it promises.

XIII Death

Here, Death means a rebirth and a renewal. You have overcome the mourning period after a separation, have meditated and healed your wounds, and eased your pain. You can now look forward to the future with a great deal of confidence. Any change is something like a little death, in that you need to come to terms with the past in order to be free for new things. Time for mourning is important, for it is part of the healing process. Now you are following the flow of life and are not allowing yourself to be deterred by the difficulties of the past. Victory and triumph are the rewards.

In a new relationship, this card means a distinguished beginning. If the previous relationship was unhappy, you have now drawn a winning ticket, for you feel equal to the challenges. New self-confidence also comes as a benefit of this relationship.

You may have given up hope for a new and successful relationship, yet it is here now.

XIII Death Reversed

You see the negative side of things in each and every instance, and have a self-destructive tendency. There is also a complete indifference as to who is hurt, as long as you are not. In a relationship, you have not progressed, but simply live side by side with your partner. This seems unimportant to you as long as your personal advantages remain intact. Any sensitivity in relation to your partner has been lost, and love has been buried under egoism. From pure self-interest, the connection to a new partner is lost.

If you are alone, you have given up hope for a new relationship and are filled with self-pity. You have also shifted the blame for your unhappiness onto others. Such behavior will drive away any partner. It is essential to change these views, for you are contributing very actively to your own unhappiness and cannot escape this responsibility.

XIV Temperance

The two cups indicate, through the constantly flowing waters (with no drops lost), that you can handle your feelings well. In a relationship, the couple orchestrate with each other very well, are contented with their lives, and with that which they have created for themselves. They act emotionally, are ready to listen, and will try to get rid of problems before they become heavy burdens. Harmony is extremely important to them.

TEMPERANCE.

The Temperance card also indicates—if you are following a professional path—that now is a good time to discuss a change of career with your partner or to put a new idea into practice. A planned move or even an apartment hunt stands under a favorable star.

People who are newly in love often exchange tireless caresses and enjoy spending romantic hours in companionship. This card symbolizes for them the grand feelings that are experienced as, for example, they enjoy the first rays of sunshine on a secluded mountaintop or stroll into the sunset.

XIV Temperance Reversed

Feelings cause confusion, for you are not handling them well, and perhaps do not truly know how. You may be suffocating your partner with constant demands for proclamations of love, or giving feelings free rein, without being concerned about whether he/she is equal to this emotional exuberance. If the anticipated reaction from the partner is missing, you will feel rejected and try something even more intense, but the result will be the same. Maybe the partner is overtaxed from too many of these emotional outbursts that alternate with proclamations of love.

In a new relationship, you immediately want a promise that it will last for ever, without taking the necessary time to get to know each other. A good relationship wants to have

Temperance shows that romance and cuddling are the hallmark of the new relationship. The couple ride off hand in hand towards the horizon. As partners, they live in harmony, mutual trust, and consideration.

time, yet this is what you do not or cannot see. Perhaps you have faced too many failed relationships; but in any case, the air to breathe is taken away by this love.

XV The Devil

THE DEVIL.

This card represents the fear that you feel yourself afflicted, which exists only in your head. If you take a good look at this card, you will discover that you can free your-self from these imaginary chains, if you only wish to do so.

On the one hand, the Devil symbolizes the fear of a new relationship. An earlier relationship has not turned out well, and you are now afraid that a new love will end as the last one did. You long for togetherness and love, but run away if it seems possible that it could come true. On the other hand, perhaps you have a fear of reality. You may have fled too often into your dreams of ideal love, and are afraid to show your feelings because you do not want to get hurt. If you don't admit to these feelings, the fear becomes larger and larger until at last it overcomes the wish for a relation-ship. You could even suffer from an unconscious inferiority complex.

How often are you afraid without knowing precisely why? This floating fear is symbolized by the Devil. You can easily free yourself from it, if you want, for the shackles of this fear are only loosely attached.

If you are in a solid relationship, you may be afraid of your partner. If that is the case, try to analyze these fears and—if there's a good reason for it—seriously consider a separation. No one should be given the power to force another into fear and helplessness. Take a look at the shackles round the necks of the couple on the card. They are very loose. This means that you can shake off these bonds easily, if you want to and summon the will to do it.

XV The Devil Reversed

You have freed yourself from your inner fear and feel like a new person, for you have successfully come to terms with your difficulties. You may have found the courage to free yourself from the oppression of a difficult relationship. It feels good not to live in self-produced fear.

With a new relationship, you realize the need to take it slowly and not let yourself be forced (by fear) into any over-hasty actions. You have developed enough self-esteem to know that you don't have to rush into anything.

XVI The Tower

A new partner has stepped into your life, and it has turned into a complete mess. Perhaps you were already of the opinion that life had no more surprises to offer, yet now everything appears completely different. Life is ordered entirely anew. The Tower pulls down old structures.

THE TOWER.

If you are living in a stable relationship, it may mean that you are giving it up in order to enter into a new one. A lightning bolt has crashed into your life from out of the blue, and your previous life has fallen out of joint; nothing is as it was before. You know that you are going to rush once again into the risk of love. In order to do that you must separate from the old relationship, but you are prepared to face the sad consequences.

Such liberation has its positive side as well, for it is a release of the old ways. You and your partner may have been living emotionally apart for some time, so that a drastic step is necessary in order for both partners to get the chance for happiness in a new connection. In spite of all that, it is still difficult when you are faced with the ruins of a relationship.

One look and you are struck as if by a bolt of lightning. Life will never be the same. The Tower symbolizes just such a dramatic transformation. Everything that has been loved and cherished up to this point is turned on its head.

XVI The Tower Reversed

You have shut your eyes to your own problems and have firmly sealed the door to your fellow creatures, taking refuge in an ivory tower. Yet relationship problems will not dissolve into air through these tactics: they will have to be resolved. You cannot always hide from life and its troubles. Look around. There may be nobody left from whom you have to hide; your partner has already gone. You are making your life unnecessarily difficult, since you are living in the past and in your ideal world. You are not able to picture a future under any other circumstances. But in order to lead a fulfilling life, you need to stand up to reality.

XVII The Star

THE STAR.

You are an idealist. In spite of all the difficulties and all the adversity that you have experienced in life, you firmly believe that you will find a new partner once more. This card tells you that your confidence is justified.

In a relationship, problems are resolved to your mutual satisfaction. If you are hoping for children, this wish can be fulfilled now. You are completely committed to the relationship. There is nothing more beautiful than to be there for your partner.

If you are in a new relationship, it will develop just as you had imagined it. You suit each other well and have common interests and plans for the future. In an atmosphere full of confidence, the relationship can develop in calm and leisure. Love grows and strengthens itself.

XVII The Star Reversed

The Star describes idealism in its most beautiful form. You are time and again prepared to give your life a new lift, undeterred by set-backs. Love grows and strengthens itself.

In your relationship, there are continual disputes and differences, and you really don't know why. The partnership is without any particular warmth, and you feel very much alone. All the feelings that you show for your partner appear to sink into nothingness. It may also be, however, that you are responding only reluctantly to the advances of your partner. Ask yourself whether love still exists or whether you are staying with your partner only because you are afraid that you won't be equal to the stress of a new life alone. Take some time out in order to draw on your strength.

Your wish to commit to a new relationship will remain an

illusion. You are fooling yourself about these desires and have taken refuge in your dreams. The beloved will not come because he/she is not interested. Try to find your way out of these deceptive hopes and return to the reality of life. You will only find a new partner in reality.

XVIII The Moon

THE MOON.

The Moon promises mystery and uncertainty at the same time. This card points to the hidden and the indefinite, as well as to the unconscious and its power, which is sometimes so difficult to understand.

In your relationship, you feel that something is not right. You know that the partner is deceiving you, but you have no proof. You are uncertain and desperate. Perhaps you yourself are the one who is deceiving the partner and hiding this fact behind lies and intrigues. Perhaps you would like to hang onto your partner until the new secret love delivers what it promises. You don't want to show your hand until you are secure in the new situation. This hide-and-seek game cannot be maintained indefinitely; at one point the truth will come to light. In this relationship, there are intrigues on both sides. You have not expressed what has been bothering you, having given up speaking about your feelings or uncovering your emotions. In this way, you have built up a protective wall behind which you are hiding. This wall, however, is also a prison. Even the walls of Jericho had to fall one day.

A new relationship is standing on unsteady ground. Perhaps you are already in a relationship beside the one with your present partner, which you do not wish to give up, or the previous love has not been granted closure and you are mourning the old life. Therefore, the new partner doesn't really have a chance. He/she will truly serve only as a stopgap, until you decide what you want.

The Moon conceals much of a love that would rather not be seen in the light of day. It promises uncertainty, as you will break through the darkness only with great difficulty. This symbolizes the relationship in which you find yourself.

107

XVIII The Moon Reversed

You do not feel right about your relationship, but do not have the courage to express your feelings and face the consequences. So you lie to yourself and to your partner in hopes that things will get better all by themselves. However, you know that this won't happen without your doing something about it. So you are walking through life without a true goal and with no idea of how it should go. We are not victims, however, but the creators of our lives. If you don't find the courage to take your life in hand, you will not find fulfillment. Passivity and indecision need to be overcome in order to shape your fate anew.

XIX The Sun

The Sun indicates that you can become reborn from the ashes, like the phoenix. You have gained new self-confidence and found the courage to show the world who you are. You no longer need to hide behind a mask. You have taken your life in hand, made some difficult decisions, and come out a winner. A relationship shines in bright glory. Your partner is virtually overwhelmed by a great deal of cheery good nature. You fit together well, and this gives your life together a certain zest. Happiness prevails, and also satisfaction in the fact that you have discovered your partner again. Mutual trust is established once more. If the children are grown up and have left home, you now have the peace to fall in love with each other all over again.

A new relationship is pure sunshine: you fit well together and are full of confidence and the joy of life. This is surely the partner with whom you want to spend the rest of your life.

Like the phoenix that rises from the ashes, you are born again with the card of the Sun. All difficulties are overcome. A married couple will discover themselves anew. Love, romance, and confidence shine in fresh glory.

THE SUN.

XIX *The Sun Reversed*

Here comes a fraud: the person who would like to impress you with his/her achievements and accomplishments and is surprised that the proper respect is lacking. This person may believe that having money automatically guarantees a free ride, and that external values are the only important things in life. Inner loneliness is suppressed and drowned out through activity, for it is possible to buy company; if that is what you want, the means are probably available.

Relationships do not rest upon mutual openness, affection, and trust, but rather on superficial matters; you can probably be replaced without much fuss, once you have done what is needed.

In a new relationship, there may be an attempt to put something over on you. If the person is well-off, he/she will try to impress you with money. If not, the person may delude you with false promises.

XX *Judgment*

Freedom from old compulsions, and letting go of obsolete habits and prejudices are the keywords here. You may have separated from an older, no longer working partnership, having seen that this relationship constricted life and no longer brought fulfillment. You have recognized that the two of you have lived apart and are ready to accept the consequences. You are doing this without fear, knowing that getting free of constricting structures also means becoming prepared for something new. The ending of an old life or an old perspective is inevitable and need not hinder a new beginning.

Judgment symbolizes freedom from old oppression. You have removed yourself irrevocably from old attitudes and pressures and delivered yourself into profound feelings once again.

If you are in a working relationship, then it may be that the shared life has fundamentally changed and you have gone along with these changes. Perhaps you had to give up a lavish lifestyle in order to gain control of debt, or another decision was made that broke with earlier mistakes. Possibly you are

109

JUDGMENT.

trying something that you have never tried before—maybe a trip around the world or taking a professional sabbatical.

This card says that something has become outdated and you know it. A change or a new beginning will be a positive step, even if that is not clear right away. In a new relationship, you will feel like a different person; the old self will be left behind completely and you will experience the self in a totally new way. If you hid your feelings in the past, you are ready to reveal them now, even at the risk of getting hurt. This mental liberation from old pressures will offer many new opportunities.

XX Judgment Reversed

You have squandered your talents and self, wasted time, and have not recognized the possibilities that life offers. In a relationship, you have not shown the ability to persevere and have given up when faced with the tiniest of difficulties, only to regret your decision later on. If changes are imminent, you want to keep everything the way it was before, for fear of losing control over the relationship. Yet this control had been lost anyway, long ago. You are divided and discontented with yourself, glancing resentfully at other people, scarcely able to curb your envy. This discontent is often projected onto the partner, yet at one point you must answer for your own actions.

XXI The World

The World unites all troubles and trials— and also all joys and happiness—in itself. You have arrived at the end, which is at the same time a new beginning. Profound love characterizes the relationship.

You have completed your journey, formed your experiences, and you know now that life is continuous motion. There is an ever-pending conclusion and through this an ever-pending beginning. When the end of a cycle is reached, life begins anew, enriched with the knowledge you have won on the journey.

As a partner, you are responsible and empathetic, part of a well-practiced team that mutually understands and respects each other. Trust and profound love have taken the place of great passion.

In a new relationship, you firmly believe that you have reached the goal of your desires. Your partner shares in the mutual plans for the future, and you have, therefore, a solid base on which to found a family. You are willing to take the responsibility for such a step.

XXI *The World Reversed*

THE WORLD.

In a relationship, you are confronted with a riddle: everything has worked out well until now, but suddenly silence reigns. The partner (or you yourself) has become distant and is no longer easy to reach. This needs to be talked about. Perhaps you have spoken too soon about planning a family and have forgotten to ask the partner how he/she imagines the future. All is not yet lost.

You tend to be an overprotective mother or a dominating one; in either case, you prefer that the children stick close to the family, and are reluctant to see them become independent. Are you afraid to be alone with your partner? Are you unsure what to talk about with your partner when you are alone together, when children are no longer an issue? You still have a good relationship, but lack the necessary energy to enliven things and stir up earlier passions. You need to undertake more things in common and no longer hide behind work or family.

Now you have lost the overview and don't want the children to leave the nest, says the World Reversed. Perhaps you are afraid to be alone with the partner because you don't know anymore whether you can communicate with each other. You need to talk this through.

111

Spreads

In this section, you'll find three spreads that have proved particularly worthwhile in questions of relationship: the Six-Card Spread, the Celtic Cross, and the Relationship Spread. You can of course choose any other spread as well. Select the one that appeals to you most.

The Six-Card Spread

Don't try to read a final and definitive answer into each posed question. It can be more informative to look at the circumstances behind the question, such as your own attitude and path, in order to bring about the "final result" for yourself. The Six-Card Spread offers you the chance to get more information and draw your own conclusions.

Before I show you how to get an answer to the question posed at the beginning "Does he love me?," I will explain the principle of the Six-Card Spread, which was developed by me for just such questions.

The Six-Card Spread is meant to be used to obtain clarification after the reading of the cards regarding any particular subject—a fight, for example. The card pattern is thus open, which means that it leaves unanswered the question regarding the final outcome. It will cast a lot of light on the situation, but will not give a precise answer. If you want one, simply draw a seventh card and interpret it. That will give you your answer.

Questions About Relationships

If you are asking questions regarding relationships, it is usually more informative to find out how you truly see and assess your partner or how you assess yourself, than to know how a relationship will turn out. Also, it has proven effective in the reading of Tarot cards to better understand the causes of the difficulties or misunderstandings that burden a relationship.

A partner does not always enjoy being asked about how he/she regards the relationship, even if it is a happy one. It is also very annoying to be required continually to proclaim your love, while the one who demands it cannot hear it often enough—and then tends to question and challenge it again and again.

An Open Spread

The Six-Card Spread is very flexible and can answer many questions, such as "Do I love my partner?" or "How does our relationship look?" When you are reading the cards for yourself, remember to ask about the attitude of your partner and look at the cards from his/her standpoint as well. Here are a few different possibilities for using this spread. Your imagination in experimenting with this has no boundaries.

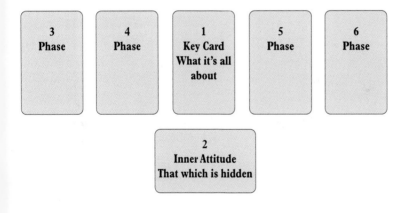

With the Six-Card Spread, you can ask, for example, about the attitude of the partner towards the relationship, even if he/she is not present. This can be done also when you're laying out the cards for someone else.

The Meaning of the Cards

- Card 1 always represents the Key Card, as well as the topic—what it's all about.
- Card 2, lying below and across, displays your inner perspective, an attitude that does not show on the outside. Perhaps you are no longer aware of the subject or have repressed it. If it does not relate to the inner perspective of a person, this card will represent what secretly lies behind the questioned topic.

113

• Cards 3, 4, 5 and 6 are the so-called Phase-Cards. They give detailed answers to the posed questions, up to the present moment.

Does He Love Me?

Here you learn how the cards answer the initial question "Does he love me?"

Card 1—Key Card—Ace of Pentacles
This card shows how "he" sees this relationship. He is rather a deliberate type, who takes his time in regard to the progression of the relationship.

Card 2—Inner Attitude—Nine of Pentacles
He sees himself as someone who has achieved something and is satisfied with life.

Card 3—Phase Card—The Hermit
He is a person who listens to his own advice. He internalizes his feelings and does not readily expose them.

Card 4—Phase Card—The Tower
Love has struck him like lightning. This relationship has completely thrown him off his old, well-traveled path.

114

Card 5—Phase Card—Four of Wands
He does not regard this relationship lightly, for it represents
the future for him.

Card 6—Phase Card—Ace of Cups
The Ace of Cups gives the answer to the question of love: the
card shows how very much he is in love.

Interpretation

If you look at the cards, you can learn the following: "He" is
a person who builds on something rather slowly and does
not hastily enter a relationship (Ace of Cups). He is perhaps
something of a loner, keeps his thoughts to himself, and
makes his decisions in stillness (The Hermit). He is very satisfied with what he has achieved in life (Nine of Pentacles).
He has been surprised and overwhelmed by this relationship;
the feelings of love have struck him like a bolt of lightning
(The Tower). He is very happy and would like to make this
relationship a solid and integral part of his life. He is in love
(Ace of Cups) and indulging in feelings which to him, as a
rather practical person, are truly foreign. The answer to the
question "Does he love me?" is therefore an unqualified "Yes."

The Phase Cards show clearly how this relationship has developed and manifested itself for "him." Tarot cards allow you to ask about the motives of your partner and perhaps put out the answers for further discussion.

What made the questioner somewhat uncertain was the
fact that he had scarcely shown his feelings. Now she knows
that he is someone who does not lightly speak about his feelings (The Hermit), though they do exist. And you can see
that he is more than merely amorous, even though he does
not speak about it.

The sum of the digits of this reading is 4 ($40 = 4+0 = 4$)
and confirms that you can build on this love.

Why Can't I Find the Right Partner?

*Ms. H., 34 years old, had been living alone for some time and
was, in spite of all her efforts, not in a position to enter into a new
relationship. Some time ago, she got to know a man whom she sees*

now and then. They go out together occasionally, but no genuine relationship has come about.

From the question posed above, the cards answer as follows:

The Six-Card Spread can be truly helpful to you, if you would like to become clearer about your own life or perspective.

Card 1—Key Card—Knight of Wands Reversed

Here is a person who appears very egotistical and preserves his advantage at any price, no matter what the cost.

Card 2—Inner Attitude—Five of Swords Reversed

Ms. H was deceived in an earlier relationship and still suffers much from this deception. That this card lies under the Knight of Wands indicates that she was deceived by the man that the Knight of Wands Reversed represents.

Card 3—Seven of Cups

Ms. H. is still quite undecided about whether she would truly like to be in a relationship. She has great doubts and fears about bonds that are too constricting; on the other hand, she is also afraid of losing her partner through her indecision.

Card 4—Four of Swords

She has withdrawn in order to draw courage. The question of ties or independence occupies her intensely. She feels herself to be an independent woman who copes with life well.

116

She does not want to live alone; however, she immediately retreats when someone shows interest.

Card 5—Two of Wands
Despite all her doubts, Ms. H. has taken the risk of sending the man of her heart a message. Full of hope and anxiety, especially as she does not know very much about him, she is now waiting for an answer. She does not know his private situation.

Card 6—Knight of Cups
The last card shows that she has chosen a man who is not interested in having a solid relationship either. He is charming, very sensitive, and therefore very attractive to her.

There is no card here to say how this relationship will work out; it is up to Ms. H herself to think about the problems described in the spread, and to shape her future.

Interpretation

The cards show that for Ms. H., her very unhappy preceding relationship is still an issue (Knight of Wands Reversed). She still feels herself exploited and deceived, has not yet freed herself from her earlier disappointments, and suffers from the loss of her self-esteem (Five of Swords Reversed). That affects her attitude towards the new relationship.

The Seven of Cups clearly says that she is still undecided as to whether she would like to enter into a new relationship at all. The retreat that she has made confirms this (Four of Swords). Now she has fallen in love and is trying to escape from her self-imposed imprisonment. She has taken a risk and sent the new man a message (Two of Wands). The Knight of Cups, however, points out that this man does not want to enter into a solid relationship. He is unwilling to commit and will most likely take off at the slightest hint of familial obligation. To Ms. H, however, he appears irresistible, because he is sensitive, and her feelings are also important to him.

The sum of the digits of this reading is 9; that means Ms. H. needs to come to terms with her past in order to successfully shape a new beginning.

Arrangement of the Future

Why is there no card that shows how it will all turn out? That is up to Ms. H herself. She needs to devote herself to the question of why it has taken her so long to come to terms with her past, together with the question of what went wrong in her previous relationship and how she herself has contributed to her failure. Once she does this, she will be able to avoid making the same mistakes in a new relationship.

How Do I See My Boyfriend?

Carol was 22 years old, freshly in love, and had known her boyfriend for eight months. She liked him very much, but had her doubts as to whether he was the right one for a lasting relationship. Her boyfriend wanted to move in with her, and she therefore wanted to know more about her feelings for him.

If you are not clear about your feelings for your partner, Tarot cards can be an unerring advisor.

Card 1—Key Card—The Fool Reversed
The Key Card tells Carol that she is very subtly opposed to moving into a shared apartment with her boyfriend. He presses, but she is skeptical.

Card 2—Inner Attitude—Four of Swords
Her inner attitude shows that she is withdrawing, and does

118

not wish to discuss the topic. She has gotten herself some space in order to think about her feelings, but her boyfriend is not sympathetic to this.

Card 3—Two of Pentacles
Carol sees her boyfriend as a man who can easily balance his hectic professional life and their shared time. This impresses her. She knows that she can count on him. She sometimes wishes that he could be less transparent and a little more exciting.

Card 4—The Hermit Reversed
She is uncertain because her boyfriend does not take her objections seriously. For him, their being together is something that was determined long ago. She finds that he looks at the relationship as a given, and she misses being courted.

Card 5—Two of Wands Reversed
For Carol, this relationship is full of too many inconsistencies—it appears to have no future.

Card 6—The World Reversed
Her initial enthusiasm has cooled a great deal. Carol does not know exactly when it started, but now she has little desire to maintain this relationship.

It sometimes happens that what we are deceived into thinking is love, is not really love. Tarot cards demonstrate this difference very well, making it possible for the questioner to see the relationship more clearly and give it a new foundation.

Interpretation

Although Carol had spoken of her boyfriend with great enthusiasm in the beginning, she now had to admit that she was plagued by great doubts. She confessed that her boyfriend felt as if he was married already after only eight months and took too much for granted. That angered her, but she had not been able up to this point to talk with him about her frustrations. The more pressure he exerted, the more she retreated. Carol had become very thoughtful, but had not been conscious of how great her inner rejection had

119

become. She did not want to end the relationship, but she knew that a conversation with her boyfriend was absolutely necessary and had to be brought about.

It is doubtful whether the relationship will last. It seems that the partners' ideas of how this relationship should develop conflicted a great deal.

The sum of the digits of this reading is 11: the number of sensitivity and insecurity; this suggests that Carol does not know how to come to grips with the problem. For her the question is whether she should maintain the relationship or start all over again.

Questions of Time

If the Six-Card Spread is questioned about a certain period of time, such as: "How will my relationship develop within the upcoming months?" then the cards show the following picture:

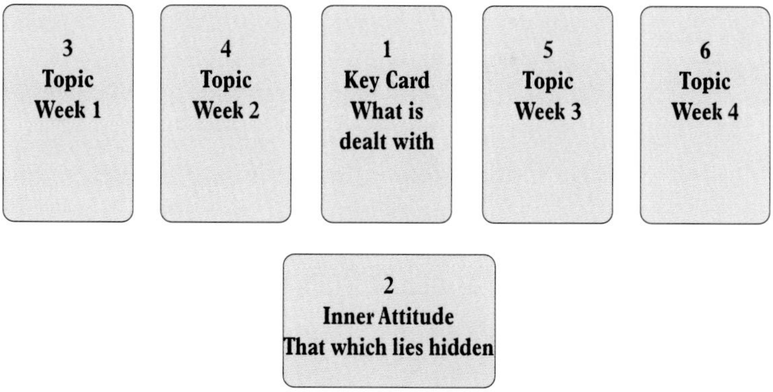

3 Topic Week 1	4 Topic Week 2	1 Key Card What is dealt with	5 Topic Week 3	6 Topic Week 4

2
Inner Attitude
That which lies hidden

It can be helpful to watch the course of a relationship over a period of time and obtain information on the kind of issues that tend to arise within the set time-frame. This time system is universally applicable.

This system can be applied to any period of time. Simply take the time frame that you have set for yourself and divide it by four. Each of the four Phase Cards indicates the topic that is of importance for that period of time.

You can use this time system for a day, a week, or any other period. The four Phase Cards each show the topic for the period of time selected. If you would like to determine the course of a day, for example, cards three and four describe the morning and the cards five and six the afternoon or evening.

How Will Our Relationship Develop?

Renate F. has had a boyfriend for some time with whom she often quarrels. They have just reconciled once more and she would like to know how the relationship with her partner will look in the upcoming month.

The cards submit the following answer:

This spread indicates that the questioner will always be the one to give in. She is unshakably convinced of the fact that she has found the right partner and is willing to do everything possible for the relationship.

Card 1—The World
Renate F. is sure that she has arrived at her heart's desire. With this man she wishes to start a family.

Card 2—The Knight of Swords
She is aware of the fact that she is involved with a very unsteady human being who cannot stand boredom and is always seeking new incentives. She believes that with him she will lead an exciting life full of surprises.

Card 3—The Four of Wands
The first week still stands under the sign of reconciliation. They will feel as if freshly in love once more and enjoy their togetherness.

Card 4—The Seven of Wands
Suspicions sneak in. Renate has not completely come to terms with a former disappointment. She also needs to take a closer look at the people who wish to influence her against her partner, in case mistrust is being stirred up by those around her. Perhaps selfish interests are being pursued.

Card 5—The Six of Swords
Everything has calmed down once more. Things have been clarified. Perhaps holiday plans are under discussion.

Card 6—The Star
Deep in the innermost reaches of her heart, Renate is an idealist and firmly convinced that her partnership will prove successful. The Star tells her that this belief is justified.

Interpretation

Even if you lay out the Six-Card Spread for a certain stretch of time, the Key Card will always display the topic that is most important for the questioner at this particular moment.

In this case the cards confirm that the partners have reconciled once more and that Renate very firmly believes in the relationship. On the one hand, however, she feels very uncertain because of the unsteadiness of her partner; on the other hand, she likes being kept on tenterhooks by him. As we have seen, the peace made between them will last for the first week, but will be overtaken by mistrust in the second week. The Six of Swords tells, however, that the relationship will once again be strengthened. Renate regards this man as her partner for life. She is willing to fight for

Don't fall into the trap of looking at the march of time for each week or month regarding the relationship. Doing this, you can easily forget to make your own decisions. Take the statements of the cards as personal advice, but decide independently, for you alone will have to bear the consequences of your actions.

this relationship and is full of hope that she will find a solution.

The sum of the digits of this reading is 11. This points once more to the fact that Renate is very uncertain about her partner and sometimes does not know how to act around him.

A Warning

It is very tempting to look at the course of a relationship each month or even every week. Here a precaution and a healthy understanding are necessary. You will, of course, not be able to solve your problems through the cards. If you lay out the cards every month in order to see whether the relationship will take a good or bad turn, there is the danger that you will act according to the statements of the cards. Your perspective on reality can very easily be lost. Tarot cards must be seen as hints and not as the determining factors of a decision. It is only in times of great uncertainty that you will want to consult the Tarot cards using this time system. It may then be very helpful, as it will give insight into how things are working out.

Don't be intimidated if a lot of "negative" cards appear in one reading. The guiding principle should always be: "How can I deal best with these challenges and turn them into something good for me?" Therefore, please never tell yourself: "The cards have predicted that this will be a bad month, therefore, I will have to suffer this month." It would be better to think about why so many difficult cards appear and what negative attitudes of yours could be contributing to them. You may then change your attitude and with it the course of the cards.

The Celtic Cross

Another spread that has been popular for a long time is the Celtic Cross. In this spread, each card has a firmly assigned place that gives information about different aspects of the question and its answers.

- Position 1, the Key Card describes the topic we are dealing with and the situation the questioner is in.

- Position 2: This card opposes the topic and makes clear whether the current situation is supported or hindered.

- Position 3 shows how the questioner represents himself or herself on the outside or how a situation is represented on the outside.

- Position 4 is what contributes to the current situation, what the questioner secretly or unconsciously thinks about it.

- Position 5 is the present—what influences the questioner and his/her life.

- Position 6 shows future influences—the topics that will confront the questioner soon.

- Position 7 describes the attitude of the questioner in regard to the current situation.

- Position 8 illuminates how other people see the situation.

- Position 9 shows hopes and anxieties, depending on whether the cards are positive or negative.

- Position 10 reveals the "final result," how the situation will develop at last.

The Celtic Cross is a very expressive spread and highly popular. It also contains coded statements about the time frame within which the question will take place.

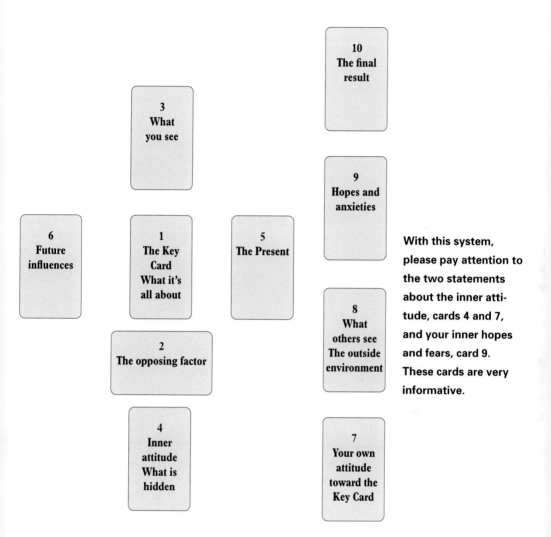

With this system, please pay attention to the two statements about the inner attitude, cards 4 and 7, and your inner hopes and fears, card 9. These cards are very informative.

How Does My Marriage Look?

Mrs. W. has been married to her husband for several years. Now she questions the cards about her marriage. She refused to develop greater insight into her relationship before the reading, but wanted to wait and see what the cards would tell her.

Mrs. W. drew the following cards:

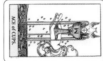

Aces are always a
positive beginning
and, therefore, are
given great
importance in the
overall statement.

Card 1—Key Card—Ace of Pentacles
The Ace of Pentacles as a Key Card tells that Mrs. W. is of the opinion that her marriage is on solid ground and that together the partners have worked hard for what they have.

Card 2—Ace of Cups
The Key Card is opposed by the Ace of Cups. This means that there is a chance of rediscovering her buried feelings for the partner after a long time.

Card 3—The Magician
At the top of the column stands the Magician: On the outside, Mrs. W. shows self-confidence and self-assurance. She

has a good grip on the fate of the family and confidence in her marriage.

Card 4—The Two of Cups Reversed
The inner attitude, the Two of Cups Reversed, reveals an entirely different picture. Mrs. W. does not view this marriage as positively as she pretends. Constant disagreements in the relationship sap her energy. She is facing her marriage very skeptically, if not already indifferently.

Card 5—The Three of Wands Reversed
Momentary influences, the present, the Three of Wands Reversed, tell that in this marriage silence rather than communication is the order of the day. For a long time, the partners have not had a lot to say to each other. At the moment, everyone does what he/she likes to do. Togetherness no longer exists.

Card 6—The Ten of Wands
Future influences, the Ten of Wands, shows that Mrs. W. will be confronted with difficult times. She will feel overburdened and possibly exploited. She should think about why this is so and whether she can learn to delegate more responsibility.

Card 7—The Hierophant Reversed
The Hierophant Reversed says something about Mrs. W.'s attitude concerning the topic. Mrs. W. has always had firm opinions of her own and does not readily accept the opinions of others. Nevertheless, she is surprised at why she is not given more recognition, which she, in her opinion, deserves. After all, she does everything for her family.

Card 8—The Three of Pentacles
The Three of Pentacles shows how the outside environment views the partners—as living in a relationship that has been established together. Perhaps a house had been built. In the opinion of others, both have created for themselves a safe and solid foundation; they are regarded as successful and happy.

If you are reading the cards for yourself, look at them and their meanings individually to start with, and then link them as a whole in an overall statement.

Card 9—The King of Cups Reversed
Hopes and fears: the King of Cups Reversed clearly shows that Mrs. W. is worried that her husband has lost interest in the marriage or is staying only out of apathy.

Card 10—The Four of Cups Reversed
The final result, the Four of Cups Reversed, shows once again a pleasant picture. The partners will find a way to get their marriage out of the rigid routine and will work hard on a real chance for new togetherness.

The sum of the digits of this reading is 3 (30 = 3 + 0 = 3), which promises a new vitality in this marriage.

The time frame of this question is about ten weeks. This is expressed by the Ten of Wands, in the sixth position. Within this time, Mrs. W and her husband should have made their way toward a better understanding of each other.

Interpretation

If you look at the pictures of the cards in general, you will notice the inner conflict in this marriage. On the outside, strength is demonstrated, perhaps because of the children or other people; but on the inside the exact opposite is displayed. It looks as if—and Mrs. W. confirmed this—the shared life has been taken for granted.

During the building of their future together, both had been very busy. By the time they got out of the woods financially, they had forgotten how to communicate with each other. They had very little to say. Mrs. W. was concerned that her husband stayed with her only out of apathy. She was no longer certain of her own feelings due to the silence of her husband and now believed that he no longer loved her.

The Key Card, and the card that opposes it, were, on the contrary, much more positive. Both people still had a lot of feelings for each other and, therefore, could still revive their love.

Furthermore, Mrs. W. had not realized that she kept her family tied to her apron strings through her stubborn behavior.

Here, the cards show that the structure of the marriage is solid, and that there are still feelings for one another on both sides. These feelings, however, have been drowned in the stresses of everyday life. It's just a matter of discovering them anew.

She now tried hard to deal with this weakness more consciously and also to get a grip on her tendency towards self-pity.

For me, the important cards in such a reading are those that show the inner attitudes. On the one hand, it became clear that Mrs. W. in her innermost feelings believed that love no longer existed in her marriage (the Two of Cups Reversed), and she felt exploited and unloved (the Hierophant Reversed, the King of Cups Reversed).

The silence in this marriage was also an expression of this inner attitude. For a long time, Mrs. W. herself had not brought any really positive energy into the marriage. And yet it was still available, as demonstrated by the Ace of Pentacles. The possibility of giving top priority to her love once more is shown by the Ace of Cups, which Mrs. W. acknowledged with delighted surprise.

How Will Our Relationship Develop?

Maria and Christopher were a young couple who had not known each other for too long but were very much in love. Maria was some years older than her boyfriend. There was hefty opposition from the ranks of the family against this relationship and Maria now wanted to know how the partnership would develop.

How a relationship will develop is a question that can be well answered by the Celtic Cross. The cards not only describe your future but always your present as well, and provide great insights into it.

Card 1—The Wheel of Fortune
The Wheel of Fortune as the Key Card shows that with this relationship life has taken a positive turn for Maria. This is also how she feels about it. She confirms that she needed a long time to come to terms with the separation from her former partner, although there had been very little affection in the end.

Card 2—Four of Pentacles
What opposes is the Four of Pentacles, which tells us that Maria, despite all her confidence, is holding back on some feelings toward her new partner. She does not entirely trust her luck and would like to be sure Christopher feels as deeply for her as she does for him.

Which card indicates the time frame of the question, and what do the hidden numbers tell you about the overall situation? Form your own opinion before reading the interpretation.

Card 3—The Sun

What stands above is the Sun, showing that the two present themselves on the outside as a bright couple who fit together well. They convey to others their certainty of being the right partners for life.

Card 4—Page of Cups

The inner attitude is revealed by Card Four, the Page of Cups. While Maria regards Christopher as very much in love, she also judges him as somewhat naïve. In her opinion, he is a little too idealistic, and she is, therefore, uncertain as to whether he wants to take up the responsibilities that a serious relationship brings with it.

Thus, she is uncertain about whether he is indeed the right man for her or whether she has to deal with a new disappointment.

Card 5—The Four of Cups

As shown by the Four of Cups, Maria has emotionally retreated from Christopher. She knows that he has deep feelings for her, but she is not certain whether she wants to accept them or not. This behavior makes Christopher uncertain as well.

Card 6—The Page of Swords Reversed

The future is the Page of Swords Reversed. There will be someone in the future who may be interested in causing this relationship to come apart. This person will do his/her utmost to reach this goal and will not stop at using unfair means either. Maria thinks that it might turn out to be her exboyfriend who has not yet accepted her separation from him.

Card 7—The High Priestess

This card provides information about Maria's attitude towards the Key Card. She gets along extremely well with Christopher. They are on the same wavelength; when one starts a sentence, the other is able to finish it. She has the feeling they have known each other for a very long time, and there are incredibly beautiful, never before experienced feelings of togetherness and familiarity.

Card 8—The Ten of Wands Reversed

The Ten of Wands Reversed shows that others are of the opinion that the relationship will not survive. Maria confirms that people have told her over and over again that the relationship is doomed to fail and that she is deceiving herself. Might envy possibly be playing a role here?

Card 8 shows how much the outside environment can influence your decisions. The card gives information about whether this influence is positive or negative.

Card 9—The King of Wands Reversed

The King of Wands Reversed shows Maria's desires and hopes. She is afraid that Christopher could turn out to be really inconsiderate. As she experienced this in her previous relationship, she has not been able to get rid of that fear entirely.

Card 10—The Hierophant
The Hierophant as a final result is very hopeful. It shows that the two will enter into a firm relationship. They belong together, and they will tell this to all doubters—despite their opposition.

Interpretation

Looking at the overall picture, we recognize that the relationship between Maria and Christopher has something fated about it, since the predominating cards of the reading come from the Major Arcana.

The Wheel of Fortune shows that life has taken a turn for the better for Maria, but she does not believe it yet and torments herself with self-doubt. Since Christopher is younger, she sees him as a small boy who is playing with love; this does not do justice to Christopher. Also the people in her outside environment do everything possible to convince her that the relationship will not endure. Maria might listen less to other people and more to what the High Priestess tells her—namely, that the good relation that binds her to Christopher is real. Also the Hierophant promises her that she can trust in her new relationship.

It will help if she tries not to confuse her past with her present, so that she can give her new relationship a chance for growth.

The sum of the digits 9 (54 = 5 + 4 = 9) confirms that she has to come to terms with her past in order to experience a happy present.

The time-frame amounts to ten weeks, for the Ten of Wands Reversed holds the eighth position. That means that this relationship will strengthen within the period of ten weeks, as described by the Hierophant.

> When we enter a new relationship, it is often the case that we have not entirely come to terms with the previous one. If we do not want to drag old luggage into the new relationship, we will need to learn to let go of pains and old anxieties.

The Relationship Spread

If you want to see clearly how you are behaving in a relationship or how your partner feels about you, you might use the following spread, in which cards may be drawn by both partners together or by one alone. It displays both the inner and outer circumstances that prevail in your relationship and also the unspoken wishes you might have concerning this partnership. This spread can be applied to relationships of any kind.

The Relationship Spread shows no final result since in relationships the "final result" is ever written anew, through disputes or reconciliations. It uncovers circumstances,

Two people in a relationship do not always show their true faces. Perhaps one fears that the other may not want him/her as he/she really is and, therefore, pretends to be someone else. The Relationship Spread allows you to identify the discrepancy between appearance and truth and offers you a chance to build your relationship upon honesty.

```
1                              2
How she                       How he
reveals                       reveals
herself                       himself


3                              4
How she                       How he sees
sees him                      her
                9
           What it's all
              about

5                              6
How she                       How he
regards the                   regards the
relationship                  relationship


7                              8
Her desire of                 What he
the partner                   wants from
                              the partner
```

133

injuries, or attitudes that you might never have suspected of your partner or yourself. This spread can and should be a call for dialogue.

• **Card 1 and 2—Presentation**
These cards tell how each one acts towards the other and what is presented on the outside.
• **Cards 3 and 4—Picture of the Partner**
These cards tell how the partner sees you.
• **Cards 5 and 6—Assessment of the Relationship**
This shows what the partners think about the relationship or how they look upon it.
• **Cards 7 and 8—Desires of the Partner**
These cards show what each person desires from the relationship and is perhaps not able to say aloud.
• **Card 9—What It's All About**
The ninth card shows the topic of this reading.

Does He Have Deeper Feelings for Me?

Melanie, 29 years of age, has met a man with whom she has madly fallen in love, Andrew, 38 years of age. He is certainly amiable and nice to her, but she regards him as unsteady and does not know where she stands.

Card 1—Judgment Reversed—How Melanie reveals herself
The cards show a woman who struggles with her destiny and mourns lost possibilities. She is very dissatisfied with herself and her life.

Card 2—The Fool—How Andrew reveals himself
He enjoys life a good deal and is always up for new adventures; he also likes to take risks without thinking very much about the outcome.

Card 3—The Eight of Pentacles—How Melanie sees Andrew
After having been single for a very long time, and even after

The Relationship Spread shows in its line-up how he acts, what he thinks, and how he visualizes the relationship. This is a system that you can lay out for yourself in case you want more clarity about your own motivations as well as those of your partner.

As you can see, the questioner has completely different expectations of the relationship than the partner. She would like to have a firm relationship; he is not at all committed to that.

having given up hope for a new love, she believes that she has found a person with whom she can find happiness.

Card 4—The Seven of Swords—How Andrew sees Melanie

He is aware that Melanie is imagining his feelings for her, which are actually non-existent, at least in terms of intensity. He is certainly very nice to her, but she is reading too much into his behavior.

Card 5—The Wheel of Fortune—How she sees the relationship

For Melanie, the relationship that is developing with Andrew is like a glimmer of hope. All the problems that she has with herself and her life fade away in the shining glance of this relationship. She has gone through difficult times, but in this relationship she can gain self-confidence once more; at least, this is what Melanie hopes for.

Card 6—The Four of Cups Reversed—How Andrew sees the relationship

Andrew is willing to let himself in for the adventure of a relationship. He was perhaps single for some time and is now enjoying the pleasures of a relationship. He has come to terms with his feelings and knows that he has to make compromises once in a while for the sake of the relationship.

As is often the case in a relationship, expectations and their fulfillment do not match, because the partners are not voicing what really moves them. Melanie is willing to subordinate everything to the relationship.

Card 7—The World—What Melanie desires

She would like to have a relationship into which peace enters, in which the partners treat each other with understanding and respect, and in which circumspection and sensitivity prevail between the partners; she also hopes for a relationship that will last.

Card 8—The Eight of Wands—What Andrew desires

He wants more personal freedom. On the one hand, he would like to have a relationship, yet on the other hand, he does not wish to be confined. He wants to live his own life in which he can pursue his interests without always having to account to someone for his actions. Melanie must understand this.

Card 9—The Queen of Swords—What it's all about

We are dealing with a very independent, self-confident woman who relies much more on her reason than on her heart. This is a woman who views a relationship critically, since she has suffered from many bad relationships. Despite her insecurities, Melanie loves her independence and her freedom to decide.

Interpretation

Looking at the picture, we realize that Melanie views this encounter as a rather fateful one (Judgment Reversed, the Wheel of Fortune, the World). For her, Andrew is the way out of her loneliness. Melanie has fixed all her hopes and desires on this man.

Andrew does not see this whole relationship issue in such a rigid way. He likes to get into ever new adventures without having to know the outcome at the start. He has the incentive to see what happens next. He is aware that Melanie is reading much more into the relationship than exists on his side.

He finds her nice, but there is no great love to speak of with him. He, however, does not illuminate her about his feelings either. He is enjoying entering the relationship with her, particularly since he has been single for some time. Melanie, however, limits him too much with her demands. He desires more freedom. They see this relationship from entirely different perspectives. Melanie hopes for an escape out of her loneliness, yet she must cure the pain from her previous relationship all by herself. Andrew is not responsible for her happiness. She needs to get rid of her self-pity and, if she wishes to hold onto Andrew, distance herself from him. She will have to come to terms with the fact that she is not the focus of his life and that Andrew does not share her concept of the relationship.

Very interesting is the ninth card—the topic—the Queen of Swords. It shows the independent woman that Melanie embodies on the outside. Andrew, when he met her, felt a great attraction to her supposed independence. As he loves his own freedom, he probably did not feel threatened by this independent woman. Melanie needs to reflect once more on her strength and find her way back to herself.

The sum of the digits is 6—which shows that the desire for love and harmony is very great for Melanie, who asked this question.

Melanie needs to focus to a much greater extent on her independence in order to hold on to a person who loves freedom so much. It was this independence, which she showed on the outside at the beginning, that her partner found so very attractive.

137

Can the Problems in My Relationship Be Solved?

Monica and Thomas have been a couple for some time now, but there are constant problems in this relationship. Monica would like to know whether this is going to change or how she should deal with her relationship.

Card 1—The Eight of Cups Reversed—How Monica reveals herself

She reveals herself as a strong woman who has come to terms with the past and is ready and willing to enter a new

The cards of the Major Arcana show that the partner is an introverted and insecure man and that he is transferring this insecurity to the relationship.

138

relationship. However, she is extremely demanding and will not put up with a great deal.

Card 2—The Hermit—How Thomas reveals himself
An unobtrusive person, Thomas makes his decisions first and communicates them later to his girlfriend. He needs peace and solitude.

Card 3—The High Priestess—How Monica sees Thomas
She feels very attracted to him and has the feeling that she has known him for a long time. She is aware that Thomas would fulfill any of her wishes and that he includes her in any of his decisions.

Card 4—The Moon Reversed—How Thomas sees Monica
Thomas does not really feel comfortable with Monica; however, he doesn't have courage enough to speak with her about his concerns.

Card 5—The Eight of Swords—How Monica sees the relationship
Monica believes that she has found the man for the rest of her life, but she also knows that something is not quite right and doesn't want to discuss it for fear the relationship will break apart if she does. Thus, she feels helpless since Thomas doesn't reveal his feelings either (see cards 2 and 4).

Thomas enjoys life much more than Monica and is more optimistic. She, however, lacks the courage to express her dissatisfaction. She is still too inhibited by the experiences in her former relationship.

Card 6—The Page of Pentacles Reversed—How Thomas sees the relationship
He thinks that the relationship will not fulfill its earlier promise. For him, Monica is too dependent and too careless.

Card 7—The Two of Wands—What Monica wants from Thomas
She wants to feel as comfortable in this relationship as she

felt in the beginning. She is of the opinion that if they would only put a little effort into the relationship, they could solve their problems and tackle a life together.

Card 8—The Devil—What Thomas wants from Monica

Thomas is afraid of a final commitment and does not want to admit it. Up to this point, he has had no real luck in relationships, and constant doubts plague him. He would like Monica to dispel these doubts, but she will not be able to, so he has to do it himself.

Card 9—The Eight of Pentacles Reversed—What it's all about

This relationship is not firmly established since both regard it according to their own ideas. They do not think it essential to let themselves in for the necessary compromises that togetherness requires. They also do not wish to talk about their concerns and thus both live in the expectation that the partner will take the first step.

Unspoken expectations in a relationship often become an insurmountable problem. It would be smart to clearly communicate one's wishes to the partner, and also to pay full attention to his/her responses.

Interpretation

Here are two people who absolutely talk past each other. Both have expectations of the relationship that do not fulfill themselves for either one, although Monica is still the more optimistic one of the team. She is convinced that Thomas is the right man for her (the Eight of Cups Reversed, the High Priestess), yet she also feels that she does not really understand him. He is a quiet person (the Hermit), who cannot deal with fears and concerns (the Moon Reversed, the Devil) and hides behind a mask. In addition, he regards Monica as careless, yet does not express these concerns either. He hopes that Monica will change and then everything will be the way he wants it. The expectations for the relationship (the Eight of Pentacles Reversed) will not fulfill themselves for either of them. When inquiring about the relationship, Monica admits that she is a very independent person and

140

does not consult with anyone when going shopping or spending her money in other ways. She very much deserves it. She was surprised that this topic apparently gives Thomas cause to worry for he has never mentioned anything about it when talking to her. For her Thomas represents the strong silent type upon whom she can lean. Her previous relationship was the exact opposite and now she believes she has found a reliable partner. However, it recently caught her attention that Thomas has retreated more and more and that she never receives satisfying answers when she asks him questions. Also, arguments have been more and more frequent. For Thomas, it would be important to rethink his attitude towards his partner and to the relationship in general, or at least make clear from the very beginning that he is on the lookout for a woman who will be rather dependent on him. Monica's independence causes him feelings of great insecurity. Both of them need to sit down together and discuss their emotional life. In the reading, there are four cards of the Major Arcana, which point to the fact that the emotional sphere has to be examined. It is the inner attitude of Thomas that endangers this relationship. He is plagued by too many fears, which only he himself can deal with.

The sum of the digits of this reading is 7. This shows how many difficult emotions burden the relationship. Both sides need to use a great deal of tact when they discuss their problems. Given this new information, Monica has decided to give the relationship a last try in order to save it.

index